You May Say That I'm a Dreamer

•

(But I'm Not the Only One)

•

By

Victor Trucker

●

ISBN-10: 0985089415
ISBN-13: 978-0-9850894-1-2

• Table of Contents •

• Introduction •

With every word and sentence I typed as I wrote this book, there were seemingly numberless off-shoots of clarifying explanation that sprang up as necessity while putting said words to paper. As I captured the phantom of one idea, I found that the terms I was using were common enough, but they're only common by human standards. What I mean to say is that there are many terms and concepts that we, as humans, take for granted and assume that the definitions or symbols by which we identify them are the ones that are as well implied by others whenever we see them used. We assume that our understanding of them is in fact their true nature and is as well the sum of their content. Common things germane to this book, such as "thinking", "thought", "idea" and "mind" gravitate immediately to the forefront of my awareness. We all have but human interpretations of what these are, and at best, our understanding of them tends to be cripplingly limited to the world of form.

So I ask you to imagine the task of describing the real from within a framework of language that by definition is only suited to describing the unreal. Anything that can be communicated through the spoken or written word only has meaning within this world of form and is completely meaningless outside of this context. Therefore, words such as, "God", "Heaven", "Source", "good", "evil", "Christ" or "Satan" have no meaning in the realm of the absolute. They are but our ego identities' interpretations of the symbols through which we attempt to express that which by its very nature cannot be accurately expressed incarnate.

Given these fundamental limitations inherent to this form of communication, it is with great care that I venture to express that which is traditionally discovered first-hand. I am not presuming to change the way that anyone thinks about these things, as I believe that you will agree with those parts that you already agree with and disregard those parts that you already disagree with. However, there are many within whom these ideas are blown about like so many clouds in the wind. They are just looking for some sort of explanation that will give some semblance of meaning to their otherwise similar, but as of yet, unarranged ideas. There are as many paths as there are travelers. One traveler's path will not work for another. It will work only for themselves. Nevertheless, dialog about these paths, however limited by the language used to describe them, may ignite a spark, which will in turn illuminate within another a path that will serve them (until it doesn't). Still it is always up to the traveler to know the difference. We will be taking a very different look at paths later on in this book.

There is a lot of talk within the "new thought movement" about "enlightenment" and levels of Spirituality and Spiritual growth (now there's an oxymoron if ever there was one). Some of this hoopla is being helpful by stimulating an investigative movement in a positive direction. However, the vast majority of it is only a source of income for those who pass off second-hand information as first-hand wisdom. It also seems to me that the groups of people that comprise these audiences are only getting a fraction of the picture. This may be due in part to the possibility that these gurus and teachers only possess a fragment of the picture equivalent to that of the student themselves. Or, they are simply making their stories up based on second-hand, and in some cases, third-hand information. Many of these so-called masters would appear to have simply read someone else's book (or books), and then written their own book based solely on their own personal interpretation of the content of the book (or books) they've read. All of which may well be an interpretation of yet another's work.

What I see swirling around us in this cloud of spiritual hocus-pocus is a lot of people getting rich pretending to be master chefs when they've never actually prepared a meal nor genuinely fed a single soul. All they are doing is selling their version of an age-old cookbook that they themselves didn't even come to on their own. They found it in someone else's kitchen. As well, the recipes therein are being personalized, reinterpreted and condensed into something unrecognizable to their original content.

Much of what I hear suggests to me that the last thing the world needs is another book that just says the same old stuff with some personal twists or gimmicks from a new author. Since I have no intention of doing that, I now take this opportunity to throw my hat into this great ring of philosophical discourse.

There's so much talk about manifesting this and manifesting that, from all manner of material distraction, to monetary wealth, to new lovers. All of this feeds superficial personal desires about outward appearances and distracts us from much of the core message of the true sages. While all of the time those who claim to possess this much-coveted wisdom are at the very root of this drive for material acquisition. They are fanning the flames that create the smoke like a magician might use for misdirection. This keeps the participants occupied while the magician tends to the business of securing his own financial future. None of this is either good or bad, it just isn't helpful. There are a lot of ways to make money without preying on people's spiritual hunger.

All of the focus placed on "manifesting" has many yearning for some effortless way of obtaining every sort of material possession. These same seekers have been convinced that the reason these things don't simply come to them on demand is because they require specialized instruction in the finer art of utilizing universal laws. The laws that affect personal manifestation are the very same laws that are shrouded in mystery and mostly spoken about in generalizations. And, for a substantial service charge there are workshops and seminars where some practitioner will tell attendees a few of the ideas held to be true with regard to these laws, while coaching the students to guess at the parts that the program does not provide.

The primary thing being created from all of this "manifesting" is an income for the practitioners peddling these ideas as crucial to our ongoing happiness. We will continue to acquire their wares until we realize that the peddlers themselves do not really know the fuller, deeper meaning of these laws. The part that appears to be sad is that so many people are being spiritually scrambled amidst this philosophical whirlwind. Because of the various approaches of the many teachers and the level of competition for audience, many people wind up being swept away by the smooth sound of one or another of these marketing dialogs.

So I asked myself, "If I could offer just one thing to help level the playing field, what would it be?" I decided that if I wrote a book about what I "have" experienced rather than what I "believe" about what can be experienced, that would be a reasonable start. So I sat down and started compiling the things that I have found to be authentic and expressible through solid reasoning and livable as a daily demonstration of our Oneness. Now when I say "demonstration", I'm not referring to some circus sideshow where I change my mannerisms and voice and pretend some form of clairvoyance that is a stretch even in this perceived illusion we call universe. Nor am I talking about performing a series of silly parlor tricks. No matter how well these might serve to sway the seeking mind into pledging a healthy remittance, they are still nothing more than an empty show.

What I am talking about is what I call the resurrection from error into Wisdom. He that sees the way to a better paradigm needn't talk about it, they simply do it and everybody benefits. It is those that find all of this to be so much mystery that seem compelled to talk at length about it. The new wisdom seems to have become little more than dropping phrases and slogans to imply ones first-hand familiarity of what has only been imagined, and has not yet been directly experienced. Not everybody is ready to make the shift in their awareness that is necessary to transcend this third-dimension time-space illusion and put their wisdom into practice, but for those who are, I write this book.

To all of the points of light, and the space of
peace they extend in the darkness.

• Chapter One •

Getting Started

•

From my point of view, anything that moves a person toward an honest inner exploration concerning the true nature regarding the Law of their Being is usually an exceptionally helpful thing. However, there seems to be a flood of books being written that simply intellectualize and articulate the concepts but have yet to really focus on our firsthand experience of the Authentic Identity. These teachings are helping keep the general consciousness blindly invested in this artificial sense of ourselves and the seemingly infinite trappings that accompany it. On the other hand, these books are stirring up a more prolific sense of curiosity into subjects traditionally left to the priests and sages. For this I applaud them. But, as a seeming being unto ourselves, we can look beyond the illusion to the greater presence that gives rise to all of this imagining. We must look to a greater presence that is beyond this universe and, as well, beyond the mind itself. Even the suggestion of going

1

beyond the mind seems to lead to a slippery slope into an abyss of the unknowable. So, what is it that lies beyond all of these experiential things? A nature of being-ness that far exceeds the capacities of our human imagination, that's what (well, at least the recognition of this presence).

It seems that every day, more and more people are taking a more active role in their own Spiritual awareness, whatever form that may take. This is helpful *only* if these seeming seekers persist and move beyond the limited ideas of what these introductory glimpses offer. If so, then even the most fundamental teachings have served their purpose. Like a ringing doorbell, the events we experience draw our attention to the place where one might come face-to-face with an order of their being that, up to that moment, they have denied. It is still up to the seeming individual, the so-called seeker, to rise from their current place of comfort and open the door. This is because these books won't even approach such realms. No teaching that originates in the world of form can pierce that veil. Reality *must* be experienced first-hand as it cannot be communicated. It is like trying to explain surfing to someone who has never seen an ocean or a surf board. I could explain it ceaselessly, but until there is a shift in the listener (a shift from an intellectual understanding of the moment to being present within that moment), until they actually surf, surfing will remain a mystery to them.

In spite of what claims may be made through these "new thought" teachings, the majority of them remain superficial and external, only skimming the surface. The primary concern seems to rest with wealth, affluence and abundant surroundings. This is neither good nor bad. However, it serves little more than to distract us from meditating on the current moment. Few of these texts will clue one into what awaits them on the other side of that door. This issue is often sidestepped by simply alluding to some idea, usually just partial in form, and specifically fashioned to invoke one's trust in one or another preferred path of teaching. This method may insure that many will buy the next book, or attend the next seminar, but it will almost certainly fail to answer any of our pressing questions. It simply restates the questions in different form. *Surfing* will remain a mystery.

This, of course, begs the question, "What is Truth?" The Truth cannot be known while incarnate, only its reflection may be contemplated in terms that we may comprehend. The Truth is simply so vast and incomprehensible to us while incarnate that we don't have the slightest notion or framework of reference points to even begin to understand it. The Truth is that which pre-exists opinion, belief and knowledge. Truth is the source of Wisdom, and Wisdom is the Authentic Identity – not the ego identity that we experience in this artificial place of our imaginings. When someone tells you that they have found the Truth, smile at them and say, "That's nice", and wait to see what it is that they are going to try to sell you (or just move away slowly). The words will generally sound quite convincing, but the contents will leave an emptiness shrouded in vague meaning. This allows for impromptu adjustments when a deeper explanation is requested (back peddling). This type of wisdom is incomplete and unfulfilling, as it leaves too much to the imagination, and it is the imagination that we use to fabricate the emptiness we are trying to free ourselves from in the first place. When I use Truth with a capital "T", I am referring to "the" Truth. When I use truth with a small "t", I am referring to what we hold as true in the world of form.

Wisdom is not the result of learning. Wisdom preexists all learning just as intelligence preexists all consciousness. Every phenomenon comes without learning or wisdom (with a small "w", meaning man's wisdom) and the mere accounting for it is all too often labeled as "genius", or at the very least "knowledge" at the human level. This "genius" looks at effects and traces the phenomenon back to some perceived cause. It then reduces the investigation to some sort of physical description. As I understand it, this process is called "science" – therefore, science is the "natural man's" wisdom reduced to practice. Has this become the idea? Are we to live and express through transitory wisdom and localized truths, truths that take their meaning from the opinions and superstitions of the outside world of form? While these local truths provide what we believe is an accounting of the phenomenon we call universe, in the absolute they are transitory and have no meaning.

What I see as being more helpful here is to provide as authentic an explanation of the essence of "Source" or "Creator", "God", "Spirit", "Man", "man", "mind" and "universe", as I can. Remember, if I'm using words, I'm using symbols. If I'm using symbols, I'm using ego; the symbol *from* which all subsequent symbols project. So, I wish to remind the reader at this point that these explanations are diminished, as I stated earlier, by the limitations inherent to the framework of language that conveys them. Therefore, at best they only serve as a poor substitute for real communication.

The only points throughout this that lend themselves to speculation are those that, by extension, would reasonably follow to an obvious conclusion. That is to say, where the outcome or explanation of any given experience, circumstance or event is, at least seemingly self-evident. My aim is to go beyond the recipes, beyond the cookbook and beyond this universe. This is because I am less interested in the projection than I am in the projector.

Some of the current teachings are clearly inspired to some degree. There are a few of the voices in this so-called "new thought movement" that appear to ring out from first-hand experience; heart-felt and genuine in their teachings. Many of these epiphanies came to their perceiver through great hardship and/or personal loss that forced an inner re-evaluation. For in those times of turmoil, cast like a rag doll into this raging ocean of consciousness, the only raft that will safely stay afloat is authenticity. All else is just clutching at straws and will eventually be crushed and fragmented against the unforgiving shores of the ego identity; the same rocky shores that gives birth to the source of all our fear and suffering in the first place – separation.

These brave few, however, clung to their raft of authenticity and managed to paddle back to awareness intact. The impression that their ordeal left them with was so great that they were changed from the innermost to the outermost. What these rare few have found is that the innermost and the outermost are but a dream within a dream. They have begun to awaken within the dream through the authenticity they have glimpsed carried in on the back of these ordeals. I don't know if they would agree that the Authentic Identity is the Dreamer or that we are all but the one ego's fragmented points of operation and merely players within the dream. Nor do I know if they would agree that it is the ego thought system that has allowed the confusion between the players and the playwright. However, I do feel pretty confident that they would all agree that the ego nature is not who (or what) we really are.

Each of our perceived individual lives are much like these "awakening" experiences even though we often fail to recognize this to be so. Each of us faces the raging ocean of consciousness knowing only the raft we have fashioned from the beliefs to which we cling. We are then summarily thrashed about by the opinions and error of the world which I refer to as the "natural man". This natural man sees itself as a "body" operating in an external world that is spontaneously provided by nature. This "natural world" is what I refer to as the dream, or more precisely, the nightmare. This isn't even the shadow of our being; it is the projection of a fragment of a thought in a nightmare of our own imagination's imagination. In this natural man reside error, ignorance and superstitions in things far more horrible than anything that nature could ever produce.

The realm of the natural man is what we perceive as matter and energy. Into this matter and energy we place all of our hopes and earthly desires, and into this dream we assign life – here in the body, in the physical. This natural man finds it difficult if not down right impossible to truly imagine life beyond form.

The counter-part to this natural man is what I call the "Resurrected Man" or "Spiritual Man", which is the original idea of Man outside of the body, outside of the universe. That is to say, the authentic presence that is back of us, and to us, appears trapped as a refugee observer within this dream/nightmare. This Spiritual Man is our Wisdom, our Authentic Identity, which is Infinite and inextinguishable, into which we are gradually awakening from this dream of separation and torment. It knows no limitations, no disease, no death, and certainly no separation from Source. When I say "Authentic Identity", I don't mean an identity at all. I simply use the term because there is no other way to communicate any of this without some sort of agreed upon symbols. There is no identity, as any identity implies a duality, for to have an identity there must be something that is not self to identify against.

We look upon that which we generously refer to as our human mind, and to one device we assign the qualities of consciousness, intellect, objectivity and individuality, and to another we assign the qualities of sub-consciousness, super-consciousness, and our divinity. Some call this unconscious quality the soul, some call it our spirit and others call it the entity or the "higher self", but in each case they isolate and define it as an independent existence uniquely delineated against the backdrop of infinity. As pleasant as they all may sound, these definitions do little more than keep us locked into this idea of individual selves.

This idea of a separate self keeps us bound as victims in this imagined universe which itself is nothing more than a symbol of that same idea of separation. Like a fractal, it matters not from what level you view it; the underlying idea always remains the same. It is an expression or symbol of separation and duality – "good and evil", "right and wrong", "perpetrator and victim". Until we can release the perceived need to embody these ideas, we will remain imprisoned within this nightmare serving *it* with our every thought.

These object symbols, both great and small, are in their entirety, fabrications of the ego thought system, one and all, with no exceptions. None of these represent our Authentic Identity. They are the aspects of the ego identity that allow us to maintain the illusion that we can hide from the true nature of our being. They keep us distracted from seeing the one simple truth that will instantly put us at liberty – the fact that we are already free. Not here in this place we call universe governed by our thoughts, but in the state of Perfect Oneness in Source. A being-ness that in reality we have never left. It is only in the illusion of our imaginings that we appear to have made a separate place or being-ness. Only a divided mind can foster such illusions. Even so, it remains but an infinitesimal idea within an infinitesimal idea, a thought within a thought, and it has agreed to believe that it is unique, independent, separate and special. The thought has agreed to believe that it is the thinker. In other words, it believes *it* is its own source.

There is so much metaphysical chatter about the qualities of consciousness and mind. To these, the teachers and gurus tend to assign the Divine that they perceive to be our Authentic Identity. Nothing of this universe is of our Authentic Identity. All of it is an illusion bourn of an imaginary self imposing an imaginary sense of separation upon all it can imagine. Everything in this third-dimensional, space-time universe, including the universe itself, is nothing but a series of symbols of the one idea of duality or separation. How we perceive these symbols is but a construct of the tool we call consciousness in the medium of mind that expresses the duality through what we experience as form. The five physical senses are made up by the ego and serve only to reinforce the ego identity by constantly bearing witness to separation, individuality and objective reality.

Allow me to offer an explanation. Consciousness, by its very nature, is the most fundamental expression of duality in that it requires, at the very least, two components to maintain the appearance of its own existence. It requires an active component, and a passive component. It requires something to be conscious and something to be conscious of – subject and object. So I tell you, no matter how beautifully designed or elegantly portrayed, the mind as we know it and the consciousness it appears to possess are but constructs within our illusions. They are artifacts, effects, not causes, and by no means are they the Authentic Identity in and of themselves. They are reflections within the idea of separation – the ego thought system's *substitute* for the Authentic Identity in the form of what can best be described as a dream within a dream ... It is an idea that took place in the same way that all ideas take place, in its entirety, instantaneously, beginning middle and end. The idea and its completion occurred simultaneously.

So, as I address these issues, please bear with me as I will be required to make use of some terms and phrases that support the reality of separation, duality and individual identities. There is no way around this, as the language and mental conditioning that we currently embrace has forged the reality we experience. It has as well forged the means (symbols) through which we experience and communicate it. These tools that we use to investigate this reality are therefore tailored to validate and confirm the self-same system that appears to have spawned them.

We have been led through the ages to believe that there is a "path" we need to be on, and a level of discipline to achieve. We have been convinced that it is a disciplined spiritual path to *enlightenment* of all things. So, this begs the question: "Where or what is this enlightenment, and how is it to be acquired?" It is thoughts like this that keep us forever looking *there* rather than *here.* Our ceaseless pursuit of whatever it is that currently sits at the top of our list of pursuits keeps us from being present to the moment.

We are continuously fed the belief that there is this "self" (i.e. "me") that for one reason or another, needs improving, and it is our responsibility to implement this improvement. Almost everything that you think you know about yourself is second-hand information, and what is more, it has most likely come to you from people who didn't know who *they* were in the first place. No matter what it is that we think we are, or that we are capable of thinking we are, it is NOT US. What we truly are cannot be thought (by us).

We repeat the past because we fail to learn from it. We fail to learn from it because we do not question it. We tend to simply accept into fact that which is given us by those whom we trust. It's like the story about the young woman who invites her mother to dinner one night and, knowing it is one of her mother's favorites, decides to serve an oven roast. As the young woman prepares the roast, her mother notices that her daughter cuts two inches off of the end of the roast before seasoning it to cook. The mother asks the daughter why she cut the end of the roast off, and the daughter responds: "when you taught me to cook, you always cut two inches off of the end of the roast that is why". The mother responded to her daughter stating: "Yes, but I did that because I had a very small oven, and the only pan that would fit into the oven wouldn't hold the whole roast". The daughter never questioned why, she just did as those who went before did, she simply followed. It never occurred to her what the practical reason for this action might be. We would do well to examine the things we are given as knowledge and question them as to their validity, rather than simply accepting them on what we call "faith". I don't mean the things we accept like how we cook our meals or how we dress ourselves, but more the things we accept about how we perceive others, and how we perceive our self.

If all of this seems a bit ironic to you, if not down right insane, then you just might find the rest of this book interesting. If not, you may think that I am a bit ironic, if not down right insane. Either way, I promise that reading on will in no way endanger whatever it is that you perceive as your immortal soul ...

The words of John Lennon, a visionary from the 60's and 70's, sum most of it up pretty well in the lyrics to his song "Imagine".

IMAGINE

Imagine there's no Heaven
It's easy if you try
No hell below us
Above us only sky
Imagine all the people
Living for today

Imagine there's no countries
It isn't hard to do
Nothing to kill or die for
And no religion too
Imagine all the people
Living life in peace

You may say I'm a dreamer
But I'm not the only one
I hope someday you'll join us
And the world will be as one

Imagine no possessions
I wonder if you can
No need for greed or hunger
A brotherhood of man
Imagine all the people
Sharing all the world

You may say I'm a dreamer
But I'm not the only one
I hope someday you'll join us
And the world will live as one

I'm going to ask you to imagine much more than just this, but nevertheless, this is a great start. Let's take a little journey.

• Chapter Two •

The Objective and Subjective Mind

•

So then, let us jump directly into the fray and start by declaring some of the more basic symbols I'll be using to establish many fundamental premises that will underlie much of our remaining dialog. This might get a little ugly, so fasten your seatbelts and make sure that your seatbacks and tray-tables are in their upright and locked positions. Let us get started with one of the "big" mysteries, "the mind". If we can even marginally clarify this one symbol, we can answer much of the mystery that surrounds most of mankind. If you were to ask a hundred people "What is the mind?" you would get a hundred different answers. Even though the answers would bare certain aspects in similarity they would still be quite varied in content.

For instance, many I asked proclaimed that the mind is the intellect or the seat of a man's intelligence. I have heard some say that it is the mind that makes the man and that the mind is the home of the memory and thinking. Some even declare that the mind is what we *really* are. I have heard that the mind exists independently from the body from some and that the mind is produced by the activity of the brain from others. But the one factor that seems to be a common thread amongst all I have heard is that mind and intelligence are inextricably linked and that they somehow define us. Mankind puts the intelligence in the mind and matter and calls them one.

First of all, let us consider that the mind is *not* the intellect nor does it possess intelligence. Rather, let's look at it as the medium in which the intellect is given form – where the effects of thinking are made evident. At risk of over simplifying, the mind could then be considered as the idea of a framework for hosting expression. One could say it is an imagined holographic matrix that underlies what we experience as the physical universe. It is a subtle principle or idea of matter different from the common garden variety of differentiated matter we seem to experience in our day-to-day dealings. For this symbol I will simply say that it is the underlying matrix of all that we seem to experience in third-dimensional, space-time reality. Anything that can be changed is matter (illusion) or is of the underlying framework of matter. The mind can be changed, therefore it qualifies as matter. When I say "matter", I am not referring to any actual substance, but rather what we experience as substance and the underlying framework that supports that experience.

The world in your sleeping dreams seems and feels just as real as the world in your waking experience. Therefore, what you are actually experiencing at any moment has little if anything to do with the existence of an external world. In reality it is impossible to experience an external world of any kind. All you can experience are the processes of what you also experience as a brain and a mind. So you can see that what you appear to be *experiencing* and what you appear to be *experiencing through* are inextricably linked. They are in fact one-and-the-same. They are simply layers of ideas within ideas. Each agreeing that the experience of the other validates the existence of both and therefore makes the observer and the observed appear to be real and separate.

Let me offer an explanation. The mind is to intelligence what the canvas is to the painting, what the water is to swimming. It is the medium wherein the creative outlet is expressed and made palpable. The presence of the canvas in front of the artist does not foster the creativity within the artist. It is the presence of the creativity within the artist that fosters the production of the canvas in order to express itself. Such is the mind. It is, however, the presence of what is true and real that gives *rise* to that which we experience as mind. It is not the presence of what we experience as mind that gives rise to what is true and real. The mind is not responsible for the creation itself, but it is one medium in which the pseudo-creativity expresses its nature. What *we* call mind is part of the first level of the idea of separation, which in turn gives rise to the idea of consciousness, which gives rise to the idea of the ego identity. Thus, the mind is the medium or material used by Wisdom to bring about a result as an imagined form. Intelligence pre-exists both mind and consciousness. What *we* call intelligence in the world of form has little if anything to do with real intelligence.

Mind and consciousness exist only in an imagined state of duality. Therefore I suggest that both must be illusory because in reality there can be no duality. Mind and consciousness are tools or artifacts of expression, not the *cause* of it. They are tools that, if used properly, can help to awaken us to the deeper presence that is back of our seeming world of form. Although I use dualistic terms here, I am not referring to separate or different things. Mind and consciousness are "ideas" that subsist within what IS, and just as you are never apart or separate from your seeming ideas or thoughts, so it is in our deeper nature.

Along this same line of reasoning, the mind is not the thinking, much like water is not the swimming. It is the medium where the thinking takes form. Like the water of a lake, the mind is ever ready to accept activity. Think of it like a boat pulling a water skier across a lake. The cutting edge of the boat would represent the point at which the intelligence touches and transforms the nature of mind through thought, and the skier is your consciousness of the skiing (thoughts). Between the skier and the cutting edge of the boat lies the illusion of the boat itself (the body). These are tethered by a fine thread that connects the seeming consciousness to the boat (body). The Spirit is that fine line that connects the Dreamer (the Authentic Identity) to that which I call the dream, the ego identity or the illusion.

Even if the skier (consciousness) manages to get completely into the boat, from it's vantage point within the boat, the cutting edge is still not visible, and everything that it experiences there is still always in the past or behind the primary essence. So, what is experienced is always an illusion of perception, a reaction to what was, even if it seemed to be just a millisecond ago. In this way, it is impossible for the human form (or consciousness) to exist in the "absolute now" for even in the nanosecond that it takes to render awareness of just being, the now is gone, and all that is actually experienced is the seeming residual effect of what was. All that is left is its echo or reflection; a memory or snapshot of sorts.

Keeping this in mind, let's get back to our boat. The waves caused by the dynamic activity of the boat are offshoots of thought revealing the contingencies set in motion by the qualities embodied by the thought system being expressed. The skier (consciousness) is bounced around between the thoughts while they are being pulled across the water (mind) by the boat (body or ego). When I say "thoughts" here, I mean "human thoughts", that is to say, thoughts that take their essence from the world of form (universe). So, the further from the boat you are, the more susceptible to the whims of the water (mind) you become. As well, the thoughts have been interacting with each other and are distorted far more so than when you are closer to the boat. The closer to the boat that you get, the more intense the effects of the water or mind become, because each thought is less interfered with by other thoughts. At this close-up perspective, what we experience as thoughts become very powerful and it becomes much clearer to us what the boat is doing. From the more trailing perspective, you become deeply distracted into the act of skiing (pretending to be in control) and give little thought to the processes that actually make it happen. The skiing seems more smooth, leisurely and pleasant when kept at a distance, and we seem intent on keeping it that way. We continually do this in spite of the fact that it binds us like prisoners or addicts to these illusions we serve as truth.

The acceptance of the ego identity makes us reluctant to getting very close to the boat. This reluctance is also a symbol of the decision to imagine a separate self, and this idea of a self is threatened if we get into the boat for that jeopardizes the power we give it over us. It [ego] will keep us at as much of a distance as possible from any calm states in which we might glimpse our True Divine nature and shatter the nightmare. Therefore, the idea is to get into the boat where you are no longer subject to the will of the waves, the torrents of mental chatter. In the boat you will still ride on the waves, but they are now simply your tools of exploration rather than controlling factors in your experience. However, the illusion of the boat or body is still very convincing as a tangible reality, thus once we have freed ourselves from the torment of our human thoughts, all too often we think that we have "made it". We are "enlightened", we can rest now. Enlightenment isn't a destination or a goal, and it isn't something we become because we cannot become what we already are. Enlightenment is simply the recognition, or memory, of the Authentic Identity – the recognition that none of what you perceive is what you *are*; it is what our imagination is imagining we *are*. We don't, as such, become enlightened; we already are *enlightenment*. What we do is to simply come to recognize what has always been. We begin to release our attachment to the illusions of perception and remember the reality of Perfect Oneness.

Further along the lines of my analogy, all that the mainstream teaching has done thus far is to allude to a slightly more direct control of the boat. Rather than being dragged along for the ride, we are now somewhat driving or steering the boat (or body). Some would call this *purposeful living*. Even in this position of greater control, we are still at the mercy of the water and its movement, not to mention the chaos introduced by all of the other boaters racing around the lake (collective mind). Any seeming control in this place, like the world of form itself, is an illusion. We cannot exert real control on that which is unreal nor can the unreal wield any real control over us. So as long as one of us is willingly bound to this illusion, none of us are fully free.

That which we truly are (outside of space and time) is without change. It is the same yesterday, today and tomorrow. What is expressed, on the other hand, is ever changing yet is always a perfect reflection of what is embraced about this idea of an individual identity. What I mean by this is, that which is experienced is the material expression of the Spiritual connection between the Authentic Identity and the ego identity; a tug-of-war, so-to-speak, between the Reality we *are*, and the illusion we *perceive*. It's kind of like tossing, turning and thrashing in bed to a bad dream. The body's reality (one layer of illusion) is trying to awaken you from the dream's reality (another layer of illusion), but something about the dream appeals to the imagined self and thus we allow it to hold us in place. We have given this mistaken identity authority over us and tasked it with solving all of the mysteries we appear to encounter.

The so-called unfoldment process is an ever steady state of appearing to newly "become" what always is, and always has been. However, that is all that it is, a "seemingly" continuous unfoldment. It does one thing and one thing only – it fosters the illusion of dividing and subdividing the original idea of separation within the mistaken identity. This in turn expresses itself as all of the life forms and the livingness in the world of form, but it is all transitory, it is an illusion. If I may return to the boat analogy, the boat is always the boat. It doesn't matter which direction that the boat is traveling or the patterns it is cutting into the waters; these are just its superficial expressions at the level of behavior. The boat itself may even undergo changes, improvements or decay, yet the point where boat breaks water remains of the same essence. I liken this point where the boat breaks the water to the instant in which the idea of separation emerges and the artificial sense of "self" appears (directly after). The artificial self is always *after the fact*, behind the point where separation occurs. Where the tip of the boat touches the waters is always new and undivided (at that moment) lacking any presence of a separate self. Everything behind the tip of the boat is always going where the tip has already touched.

There is only one mind, and that which appears to be many individuals (ideas of self) all share in it. Many of today's gurus refer to this "universal mind" as the "higher-self". Then this "higher-self" is shrouded in mystery as though it too were something estranged from our awareness, something we need to "get in touch with". I say that your *higher-self* and my *higher-*

self are in fact one-and-the-same. The universal mind is the universal higher-self, if the label "higher-self" must be used at all. It is not *higher*, and it is not a *self*. In any case these are still ideas of an artificial self, "higher" or not. The universal mind isn't a "real" mind at all. It is the ego thought system's idea of a mind – the reflection of a mind within a mind. It has been placed in substitution of real Mind as a framework for the illusory forms of the ego identity's imaginings of separation. In this place we call universe, the closest we can get to a *real* mind is that Spiritual connection to the Authentic Identity that is mentioned throughout this book.

The universal mind is similar to a vast sea of ego driven radio waves – broadcasting and receiving on all frequencies. What appears to be the individual mind is but a thought within the universal mind that spans only a fragment of the total spectrum of the thought frequencies (this is an analogy; I'm not talking about real frequencies, that is just the simplest description). So, to each of the seeming "thoughts" of individuality, all of the other seeming fragments, or "thoughts" of individuality, appear to actually be "other" individuals. At those places where some of the fragments share overlapping frequencies, there appears to be a simpatico or immediate recognition. We say we see "eye-to-eye" with these perceived others. Either way, these seeming individual minds only express a tiny fraction of what we call the universal mind. Therefore, these *individuals* seem to be vastly restricted as to what they appear to contain at any given moment due to their limited point of view. No idea or thought can be fully equal to, or greater than, that which originates it.

The Authentic Identity is that which precedes even the universal mind and the universal ego. The universal mind and ego are nothing more than the original "I AM", the first lie ever told. The ability to, in any capacity express the notion, "I am", must certainly proceed from an objective state. To recognize any concept of "self" at all requires the concept of something which is "not self". This also calls into action the processes of the ego nature and it's classification of seemingly separate objects into that which is agreed upon as being self and that which is not self. All that is seen as not self is then arranged in order of importance according to what is liked or preferred, and what is disliked or opposed.

Lying just beyond the simple expressions of self versus not self, we are also confronted with the prospect of duality within the mind itself – the subjective and objective minds. This leads to the question, "are there two minds operating in the one man, or one mind acting in two capacities?" At first appearances, it would seem the there were two minds in the one man due in part to what appears to be two cursory functions of the mind – objectification and subjectification. If we take the old analogy of the mind as a pond of water where the shear surface represents the objective mind and the rest of the pond represents the subjective mind, we wouldn't instinctively suggest that there were two ponds. So, in the same vein, why suggest that there are two minds?

Clearly there are two aspects of the pond's water, the surface that acts as an interface between the pond and what would appear to be its surroundings, and the depths that act as storage of everything that crosses that surface. No matter how we look at this analogy, there is still only one pond – a unity of a sort. When we venture to explain our mind with any dualistic view, we separate the mind into two parts, and here is the part that fascinates me. We then claim that there is one part that we are aware of and one part that we are not aware of. It is said that there is a conscious mind of which we are aware, and an unconscious mind of which we are not aware. If we are actually not aware of the unconscious mind, then how did we identify and define its seeming existence in the first place?

Like the pond, we agree that we are aware of the surface, or the part that seems to interact with that which appears to be other than pond. While at the same time we agree that we are unaware of what is going on beneath that surface. Yet in reality, the only aspects of the mind that we are unaware of are those aspects that we *agree* to be unaware of. It's not that we are unaware of these depths, it is just that we have labeled them something else and decided that they are beyond our scope of awareness, separate and apart from us. We are rarely, if ever, willing to accept that there is something we are very aware of that is in fact our unconscious and super-conscious mind. As well, we deny that they are ever present to us in every moment.

The outward expression of the objective or conscious mind is what we have labeled our body. It is that portion of mind that acts as an interface between what we perceive to be "self" and all of that which we perceive to be "not self". The outward expression of the subjective or unconscious and super-conscious mind is everything that we have trained ourselves to *see* as "not self". Through our five physical senses, we transfer data from our seeming surroundings to what we have agreed to believe is our "self" and back again. Back and forth, back and forth, we are in a continuous feedback loop of information between what is seen as "self" and what is seen as "not self". I for one do not subscribe to this dualistic model of the mind. I see a single mind that has been conditioned to accept as real, that which it has been fashioned to resemble, and agreeing to shroud all else in mystery. Please understand that we are still discussing an illusory mind in the first place. Not a real Mind, but an artifact of the ego thought system's imaginings of what a mind is.

If you would like to better understand your objective or conscious mind, just look at your body, and I'm not referring to the shape it appears to be taking at any given point in time. Instead, I am referring to how comfortable you are with it and the information that it seems to be relaying to you continuously throughout your experiences. As for gaining a better understanding of the subjective or unconscious and super-conscious mind, just take a look at the world around you because it is the reflection of our subjective state. This is not limited to just this earth, it extends to the totality of the cosmos and beyond. According to this model, the unconscious and super-conscious portion of the mind are truly the greater share of what we call mind. Because the objective state is simply a fragmented artifact of the subconscious, it is extremely resistant to the notion that we are simply taking our existence in and amongst our own thoughts. Rather we prefer to see ourselves as independent *from* them, or as the container *of* them, never simply one *amongst* them.

So if you ever wondered if what you are experiencing is in sync with your thoughts, just look around you. What you are seeing *are* your thoughts, or more accurately the reflections, projections or symbolic representations of your thoughts. When we apply the word "thought" to what we perceive as human, we reduce the symbol to something that we can relate to in our fragmented state. That is to say, we reduce the idea of thought to a fragment of what thought really is and we call it whole. When we reduce this reality down to something that the average human can comprehend, it isn't much. So why do some people seem to see so much? It is because they don't limit themselves to the commonly held notions regarding the nature of the mind's experience here in third-dimensional, time-space reality.

Even when we use the word "mind", the ego identity automatically distorts our perception by inserting the word (symbol) "my" in front of the word mind. As a result of this, we automatically think in terms of "my mind" and "your mind". From the ego filtered point of view, whose only function is to fragment and separate oneness into a multiplicity of "things", this begins to appear as perfectly normal within the seeming framework of experience. Because of the splintered or fragmented nature of the objective mind, it is unreliable as a tool for investigating beyond what is perceived within the illusion – the dream within a dream. The five physical senses that feed data to the mind are, as well, substitutes for our real Spiritual senses, and are useless in seeing beyond the space-time experience. The senses are also fabrications within the dream and therefore are but constructs of the ego identity. As I stated earlier, the five physical senses are made up by the ego and serve only to reinforce the ego identity by constantly bearing witness to separation, individuality and objective reality.

We can learn to recognize and understand the feedback loop of constant communication with our unconscious or subjective state. We can eventually

29

forego the mind and intellect all together as tools for aiding in the shift from "self-hood" to the Oneness of the Authentic Identity. We can do this by learning to listen only to the Spiritual connection to the Authentic Identity and releasing the need to attach to any form of human thinking to guide us. We have placed so many of our hopes and beliefs in the basket of "intellect" that it sometimes seems like without it we would be unable to function. However, what we perceive as intellect will not serve us beyond this illusory world of form. Intellect will not "get us home". If anything, the intellect will keep us here, analyzing and reasoning why we need it to be safe, to be secure, and to be happy. The intellect will not bring us any of these things. It will only bring us the ideas of these things while further isolating us and separating us from recognizing what we really are. The Spirit is essentially the "voice" of our Authentic Identity which has been ceaselessly telling us that we are home – that we are a perfect unity – coaxing us to awaken to the fact that we are ONE.

Intellect, on the other hand, wants to be right. It will go to battle to prove that the seeming "self" that supports one seeming intellect is right and that any *other* is wrong. It will go to great lengths and employ extreme measures to win every battle. Much of our perceived self worth is based on our ability to be right. When we are made to be wrong, we find ourselves feeling vanquished, devastated. We then hone our intellect like a knife and charge back into battle to regain our illusory sense of honor – the illusion of rightness. The intellect is nothing more than the imagined processor that manipulates the fragments the ego identity appears to manufacture by sectioning off the oneness and labeling and categorizing what it decides are relevant portions thereof. We place so much importance on the mind and the intellect that we put the intellectuals up on pedestals and practically worship them.

We look to those we perceive to be the "problem solvers" and treat them as though they were the chosen or anointed ones. I once heard it said that "intellectuals solve problems, geniuses prevent them." Once we are awakened within this illusion, this dream within a dream, we will see that there are no problems, no intellectuals and no geniuses, only the idea of such seeming things. The time has come to stop leaning so heavily upon these self-created crutches and realize that we are not lame, nor do we depend upon these thought-form artifacts to define ourselves. We are a self-defining presence, we are a Perfect Oneness with what "IS", perfect, whole and complete despite any illusory outward appearances to the contrary.

• Chapter Three •

Source (The "Is") and God

•

This will be a relatively short chapter, due mostly to the fact that Source, the "IS", cannot be defined or described in human terms. Even to say "God is Love", is to impose a limitation on the Creator that simply does not exist. Yes, the *IS*, is the source of all Love, but it is not limited to being this, or being describable as this. I understand that one could argue this in the light of saying that so-and-so is friendly, is not to say that so-and-so is friendly and nothing else. Being that Source is ALL that is, there cannot be any limited idea produced by man that would be excluded in the All-ness that is. Therefore any and all comments of this nature become mute. In this light, I am not really going to attempt to define or describe what Source "is" (as this is truly impossible). I will, instead, spend the next few pages exploring the many misconceptions and try to explain what Source, God, the IS, is *"not"*.

For what has been perceived as thousands of years of recorded history and tens if not hundreds of thousands more years of unrecorded history mankind has looked to the skies and called upon some distant God of his own imaginings. This God has been conceived of as a distant God, separate and apart from the perceived self. In some rare cases, there have been individuals whom have come to accept that their God is neither distant nor apart from their own being but rather they refer to the very livingness they perceive, or the mind, as God. Now the talk has come full circle once again. We hear of the universal mind and the individual mind, and once again mankind is calling out to this universal mind and looking to it as "Source". We have agreed to accept it as omniscient, omnipresent and omnipotent and that we are but the individualizations of this one great mind. We haven't come very far in what appears to be thousands of years of philosophical exploration. It seems to me that all we accomplish during each cycle of seeming Spiritual seeking is to create new labels for the same old ideas. The phase of awakening has come to re-establish the core ideas, but not through seeking – through "being".

I suppose if one truly finds peace in referring to this perceived "universal mind" as God, it wouldn't necessarily be the worst thing that could happen. However, if one is insistent on calling upon the universal mind as God, the same must relieve it of the quality of originating the creative power.   The universal mind, the individual mind as well as any consciousness' that these seeming minds appear to possess are not the originators of the creative power. They are ideas or artifacts, and neither of them are source to any true creative power. They may help to focus, distribute and experience it, but they do not originate it. The nature in us that seeks to assign these qualities of creative power to either the universal or individual mind would only be serving to keep us ensnared within that self-same idea. In fact, anything that we are capable of experiencing through our five physical senses is an artifact and is wholly fiction. Our senses, which exist within the illusion, can only sense the illusion, and therefore can only interact at the level of illusion.

That which actually *is* the "Creator" or "Source" is vastly beyond any reality that we can conceive of on *any* level through *any* consciousness. This is because the same framework of symbols and ideas that contain all of our concepts fundamentally limit them as well. It is so far beyond anything we are capable of knowing while in the world of form, that we don't even have a framework of comparison to begin to grasp the vastness of its being-ness, its *IS*-ness. That, which is the Creator, transcends any need for consciousness or any of the artifacts of this third-dimensional, space-time domain.

As I have stated, consciousness, by its very nature, requires at least two components to exist on any level. It requires an active component and a passive component. It requires something to be conscious (active) and something to be conscious of (passive). That which is Creator or Source does not require such antecedent conditions to affect creation. It is beyond any and all such limitations and is most certainly beyond any real definition or description as well. Any definition or description is limited to the framework of the symbols, language and terms that make up such a description. This includes their inherent definitions, both implied by the describer and inferred by the listener. The Source has NO limitations.

The Creator-Source can't even be limited by an identity or a sense of its own being-ness. It most assuredly must simply "Be", without cause. To possess any sort of "identity" is, as well, an imagined part of the greater illusion, and another form of limitation. An identity only exists within a state of "duality" by referencing "self" in relation to something that is not "self". Therefore all sense of individual identity is the product of consciousness, which is part of the illusion, not the cause of it. That which the great spiritual traditions of the world refer to as "man" is simply one of the aspects of the consciousness that fabricates this universe in thought form.

At the moment that consciousness occurred (the sense of "I AM"), "man" saw himself as an independent entity separate from all that it perceived as not self. At that point, the idea of "man" became the idea of the "perceiver", a conditioned space of consciousness, and for an instant agreed to believe in the idea that this was in fact a separate self being apart from the Creator. The idea that the perceived self is separate and independent from Source is the so-called "fall from grace" expressed in many scriptural accounts. The advent of this consciousness is akin to the "and there was light" referenced in many religious scriptures. This reference is to our illusory "self"-illuminating light of consciousness, not *visible* light and certainly not the light of God. It is that darkness that calls itself the light.

From this point forward, the spiritual traditions of the world refer to this conscious presence as "God". This is more closely related to that which is referred to as "Adam" in the Judeo/Christian Testament than to the IS. Adam is the universal mind of consciousness, the emerging sense of a separate self, and Eve is that part of the mind we call the manifest thoughts (not the thinking, the thoughts), the part that appears to us as the material world of thought forms. Eve is the "womb of creation" in this domain, and all seeming life forms arise and take form within her. Adam and Eve weren't people, but they did imagine all of the forms that make up our experiences, including our present bodies. Adam and Eve are the foundation of the duality that currently keeps us in a state of perceived separation. They are the natural processes of a mind divided within itself – the mistaken identities. Where it is said that Adam and Eve walked with God in the Garden of Eden, even here, the God to which this refers is the Dreamer, our Authentic Identity, not the *Creator*, not the *IS*. Adam was the Authentic Identity's idea of a separate self. Adam was Man's idea of man (so-to-speak), the emergence of the ego identity.

As long as we hold to the idea that our own identity is the pinnacle of reality, we will remain in a state of perceived separation, a wholly illusory state that serves only to support its own perception. We will continue to experience death, disease, suffering and limitation as integral parts of our existence. However, this separation has never actually occurred in reality – only in consciousness' divided thought forms. It is the imagined fragmentation of a tiny speck of the Authentic Self. If Source is the only reality, everything is and must be of *it*. Therefore, it must mean we could never actually leave or separate from Source (except in consciousness). Most certainly, separating from what "IS" would simply be impossible. That which is the Creator could not have created *this* illusory universe, per-se, as it would be a direct contradiction to its own being. It is *we* that simply imagine it the same way that we fabricate the worlds in what we call our dreams as we sleep at night. This illusory universe (the big bang) was the first effect of the breakaway idea "I AM". From its inception, the one idea of separation, the one ego, has been dividing and sub-dividing the void of it's consciousness into the seeming infinite number of imagined forms within the one imagined mind.

The only begotten Son is the *original* idea – "Man" or "Christ" or "Buddha" that has remained in Perfect Oneness with Source or God and has never been, nor could ever be, otherwise. Any sense of separation is only entertained within this thought within a thought. Within this thought within a thought, an infinitesimal portion of the thought agreed that the thought itself was the reality. At that moment the thought assumed the role of the thinker – the map became the territory. It thus became the point of operation that is perceived as form, the idea of form as the physical embodiments we humans call "man". That is to say when Adam's thoughts experienced Eve, the idea of form, he (it) knew he (it) was naked or had no expressive form, no interactive body or point of operation. Through what appears as a history of unlimited trial and error, Man's *idea* of man has been expressing the *idea* of self through the *idea* of form, continuously analyzing and redefining it into its current state.

Through the division of the void of consciousness, the seeming dreaming speck within "Man" (Spiritual Man or the Authentic Identity) imagines the expression of itself through an individuated identity in the form of "man" (natural man or the idea of the ego thought system). This only served to broaden the seeming gap between the Authentic Self and the perceived self. Thus "Man's" idea of "man" is running its course through the medium of form to the sole discovery that form and all of its trappings are but

39

illusions and are purely transitory. This will inevitably lead the mistaken identity to the ultimate conclusion that what we perceive ourselves to be is not what we are, and what we are, our Authentic Identity, has never been diminished or compromised. It will also be understood that there is nothing to be gained from remaining within this idea or illusion and that this imagined "self" has no reality in itself. Nothing that we perceive here has ever actually happened, not the way we believe it has. These states exist only in a mind divided within itself, asleep to itself in a dream state of illusory identification with form or what we perceive as independent self-ness.

Everything within the domain of form is a reflection of everything else within the domain of form on some level. The only thing that consciousness does is to reflect the idea of the illusory self within reflections of the illusory self over and over like a house of mirrors. The one thing that you will never actually see here is your Authentic Self - you can see only reflections. You see only the reflections of what passes for self in all that surrounds you. Since we have agreed to believe that these things (plants, animals, houses, furniture etc.) are separate and apart from us, we no longer recognize our reflection as it is shown to us. I do not mean that the physical forms we encounter are our reflections, but instead these forms are the reflections of the "human" thoughts that we embrace about them and how these thoughts affect us.

When we see something ugly or undesirable, we withdraw from it, or say to ourselves something like "that's repulsive" or "I would never do (or be) that" or "they should be ashamed of themselves". What ever it is that arouses a reaction or feeling within us is what is being reflected back to us through the moment in the medium of form. It is our judgment of these illusory forms that spawns the belief that a reaction is necessary and that our feelings are justified. This is where we have agreed to believe a lie, and this is the distortion from where we, at some level, cry out for healing. Healing that, in reality, we do not need. Only in this false universe, in this dream within a dream, have we agreed to believe that we are somehow damaged and thus we have the need for healing. The healing is a symbol of our desire to awaken so-to-speak – to release the idea of separation that we have substituted for Oneness and return to the knowledge of Source.

Source is the only true Power, the only true Creator, and what we refer to as Creator is the dreamer within the dream – "Man's" idea of "man", the one ego nature. I capitalize the word "Man" here to represent God's idea of Man, and represent it in lower case as "man" to represent Man's idea of man. Any of the descriptions I use in this book only pertain to this place of form, and have no meaning in the Perfect Oneness in the Eternal Always. "Source", "God", "Christ", "Man", "man" and any other labels are merely symbols for other symbols that are many times removed from their original ideas. All symbols are constructs of the ego identity and serve only to negotiate this illusory state we call reality. Symbols involve definitions, and definitions by their very nature invoke a sense of separation.

Since the ego is a construct of the mind as a replacement for our relationship with Source and since it has no intellect of it's own (only that which we give over to it), we can use its own framework and tools to undo its web of falseness and free ourselves from this mistaken identity. In this way, we can release our opinions and beliefs regarding the world of form. We simply let the dragon slay itself and come full circle back to the realization that we have, in fact, never left Source. We naturally realize that this would be impossible, as no idea or thought can ever truly leave that from which it takes its origin. An idea or thought can be extended or shared, but it can never cease to be present in its originating state.

• Chapter Four •

Man and man

•

Victor (the seeming individual sitting at the keyboard typing this stuff) is not a "who", he is a "what" and WHAT "he" is, is a part of WHO "we" are. Victor is a point of operation, and collectively we are a dream or idea of "man" in "Man". Victor is an example of the idea of what we are like, a point of operation or vehicle for carrying the presence or *awareness* of the consciousness in what appears to be a smaller scale, as a reflection of some larger scale. Everything in this universe of duality is a reflection of everything else. It would be like picking flames in a raging fire and falsely accepting that each flame is an independent fire unto itself, separate and apart from the rest of the fire and thus self-causative. Where the term "Man" appears, is to reference the ONE idea of Man that exists only within Source – that which is perfect and without flaw. Where the term "man" appears, is to reference the idea of "self" that exists within the dream that is dreamed by Man (currently asleep to

43

itself).   The term "man" references the mistaken identity, the ego identity, or whatever you wish to label it. We have defined the reflection as self, sort of like confusing map with territory or menu with meal.

I once thought the goal of the universal's process of evolution was to produce a "mate", an "equal", not a servant or a slave, but an equal. Then I realized the immediately obvious flaw to this logic; there can be only "ONE" Oneness and all must partake of it. There is only one source of all that is, one source of all being-ness. Therefore there can NEVER be TWO separate and distinct anythings. There cannot be two infinities as each one would limit the other, as there would have to be a point where one ended and the other began, lest they not be separate. Nor can we divide infinity in half as there is no mid-point to that which has no end. This can never be, as it is not possible. Therefore, I now see the goal of the universal's process of evolution. It is to produce a believable vehicle that will carry and express all that it is and, more to the point, all that it is like. It's producing trillions upon trillions of individual personalities (ego identities) that are all based on, and within, its own ego's essence. They are of the same essence, the same seeming life and livingness, sharing the universal mind, consciousness and its collective illusion of self. As such, and since the universe appears to be an illusion, everything within it must share in this illusory state as well. That is to say all objects and interactions are fictitious or imagined although the experience of them may appear quite real. The universe is simply reproducing and mimicking its own image, as it knows of nothing else.

Most of the "New Thought" teachings tempt us with sayings like "whatever you can imagine, you can manifest" and "Think of it as already existing" and "Everything you can imagine exists in potential form" or "in the invisible". What they don't tell you (usually because they don't know) is that none of it is actually helpful to our awakening, and none of it is true. Some portion of our Authentic Self is in, what can only be described as, a sleep state having a dream (nightmare) – a nightmare we collectively call universe. So, yes, we can play the manifesting game. However, by doing so, we are agreeing to believe that this universe is real and we are extracting some sense of self from the idea of it. This in turn draws us deeper into the unsolvable riddle of the false universe and keeps us trapped here in our mistaken identity pretending to solve it. Everything that we manifest will be filled with the same emptiness that we are trying to escape by manifesting it in the first place. Until we realize that everything that we desire has its polar opposite included as part-and-parcel with it in a package deal that cannot be avoided, we will continue to believe that there is something *outside* of us that will complete us.

The new thought teachings claim that the law of attraction can create health, wealth and prosperity in your life. What does that mean if it's not a "life" but an idea about a life, an illusion? As well, I'm sorry to inform you that the law of attraction cannot *create anything, ever*, anyway. All of the laws of nature that stand to validate this false universe are the relations between seeming things *after* they appear to exist. Essentially, the laws of the universe define the relationships between "things" on a purely physical level. The laws naturally proceed from any state of duality, and since there can be only ONE; the laws as well are illusions or constructs within the dreamscape. These teachings have confused the laws of nature with the creative power itself, and are attempting to accomplish through intellect, and the human mind, that which can only be accomplished by God and our true nature. The true creative power does not directly create this universe. This universe is a product of Man's *imagining, not God's creating*. Therefore, I say that there is no "potential form", but that everything possible exists right now in the absolute. It is only our awareness of the consciousness of them that appears to come into, and go out of, being and creates the illusion that this universe and its seeming contents are real and ever changing.

There is no consciousness in thought. There is, however, consciousness *of* thought, but there is no consciousness *in* the thoughts themselves. Consciousness is another tool of the ego, as well as the mind, the body and our human thoughts. These tools are not what we truly are. They are simply reflections of a nature within us that expresses some of what we are like, but never what we actually are. As I stated earlier, consciousness, in its most basic form, requires two components at the very least to exist – active and passive. These qualities are found to be the defining factors in both the mind and the body as well. We speak of "my mind" and "your mind" and we express in the form of the "individual" minds. We carry this same principal over to the body – "my body" and "your body" and where my body ends, everything else begins. We accept, as a matter of course, that our skin is the barrier that separates us from everything that is not self, rather than our skin being a delicate membrane that connects our local experience of self to a global experience of a self. We have impressed these fragmented (separatist) ideas upon ourselves so believably that we now simply accept them as an implacable authority and seldom pause to question them at all. All of these ideas exist only within a framework of duality and therefore are all are fabrications of a mind divided. They are part of the grand illusion … thoughts within thoughts within thoughts all reflecting each other.

The mind and the consciousness that it appears to possess, as well as the body, are tools of machination. They are tools that the dreaming presence within us uses to affect the dream. From the purely human perspective, they are useful in exposing the falseness of this universe and the states within it to which we unnaturally attach ourselves. The term "human perspective" implies a point of

47

operation from which the dreamer *imagines* such tools, rather than a place where such tools actually exist and control or define the actions implemented by the dreamer. If left to themselves, these tools filter and manipulate the contents of perception until nothing real appears to us, and thus everything that does appear to us is unreal. More to the point, that which appears to us are but the artifacts of that which forever remains locked within the illusion of an imagined past – the echoes of what *was* an idea, never what actually *is* real and eternal.

The body is quite possibly the most powerful tool that we have imagined to perpetrate the hoax of individual existence and maintain the perceived state of separation. The body engenders both fear and desire. It engenders the fear of loss, harm and or death, and the desire for more and more of what it perceives as validating and identifying to the "self". Without the divided mind's illusion of duality, the ego simply does not exist, for there is no "I", "me" or "they" in the essential Unity. In fact, I do not exist on any level except for the Spiritual level. On the Spiritual level, Victor is only an idea and not an independent, self-causative entity. Victor is a thought within a thought within this dream within a dream.

What we are, we are already. We aren't *becoming* it. We simply *are* it. This is both unavoidable and unchangeable. What we are, we have always been and will always be. We don't become a spiritually enlightened being. What we are is beyond enlightenment, beyond mind and consciousness, even beyond Spirit. These things only have meaning in the realm of the conditioned world of form, and what *we* have labeled as life and livingness. However, a tiny portion of our being-ness is asleep to itself and partaking of this illusion, a sort of nightmare, that we are something other than complete, something less, something separate. Nothing real is ever actually changed or rendered changeable. However, that which does evolve appears to possess the potential to pass through seeming stages of recognizing more and more of the presence of that which always *is*.

We can't become what we already are. To "become" something implies a transformation from one thing into another. It would require us to stop being the one thing in order to start being the other, and what we truly are is not becoming anything as what we are is unchanging and eternal. It is a little like we're lost and wandering through an infinite mansion of numberless rooms, each having some presence of its own and each presence contributing to the presence of the whole. All of the rooms exist even if we have yet to explore them. Some outwardly experienced understanding of the greater presence appears to gain focus and resolution as we encounter more and more of what already is, and always has been, present. What is true and real doesn't come into existence according to our awareness of it. It is only the ideas (imaginings) we agree to entertain that manifest according to our consciousness of them. The Truth does not need our awareness of it to exist. It is only the illusion that requires our continuous conscious support to be invested in it in order for it to remain in focused manifestation.

What we generally accept as "man" only takes place within the realm of form. The realm of form only exists in a subjective state within an imagined mind. Therefore, we are only subject to the rules and limitations of form to the degree that we place our belief into both the realm and the rules. As perceivers rather than Creators, we subject ourselves to the role of being the victim of our universe rather than its proprietor. This "natural man", as I previously put it, is a product of the on-going illusion of perception that governs this third-dimensional, space-time framework of our apparent existence. Seeing ourselves as bodies or as the effect (ego identity) rather than the cause (Authentic Identity) we freely deny *that* which is within us, which is naturally able to transcend the limitations of our perceptions. In fact we hide from this essence or reflection of our true nature and perceive it as a threat. Thus, we remain in what appears to be a never ending cycle of birth and death, of fleeting moments of joy and devastating bouts of suffering. All of these seeming experiences are products of a dream-like (nightmare-like) state of perceived selfhood – the fragmentation of a small portion of one imagined mind symbolically shattered into the numberless rooms in the infinite mansion.

The "natural man" resides in the idea of a body, paired with the idea of a mind, knit together with the tiniest strand of Spirit, all delineated against the backdrop of a seemingly external environment. In this man, the mind and the body define the man's existence and assert the louder, more demanding, and critical voice of what appears to be self-direction. In this man, some degree of dominance appears to be fundamental to the idea of survival. We have agreed to believe that we must dominate this seeming environment, dominate all seeming other species, and even sometimes dominate what appears to us as other persons in order to finally have any peace. Peace isn't simply the absence of war; peace is a state of mind that isn't swept into becoming every event or emotion that washes up against it. Peace is what naturally fills the void left where judgment is suspended.

These dominating actions of ours are all indicative of the process of separating and categorizing all that is experienced into good and bad, greater and lesser, liked and disliked objects. Everything that can be experienced will be delegated into our ego thought system's perceived state of duality by the inherent processes of a divided mind. When there is anything that does not conform to this requisite, we will make up stories, under the guise of the ego, to condition the apprehension of such things so that they take on newly imagined meanings and thus conforming to the imposed paradigm. In this way we can process any seeming non-compliant presence and force them into compliance with our newly imagined beliefs about them. Even though such stories are mere fabrications and have no factual foundation, nor any extension within our perceived state of being (or any of its symbolic representations), they still become seemingly real when filtered through the ego identity.

These things being said, the "natural man" is more akin to a baser self, that is to say it is generally more (if not totally) ego guided than Spirit guided – it is "of the world". This is because the natural man sees himself as separate and distinct from his brothers and sisters and his environment. He fancies himself as that which is referred to as "Man" in every main religion and the deeper philosophical fields of discourse. This natural man compares everything with everything else and sets out to paint his environment with the remnants of that which passes through the fire of his judgment. The natural man exalts the body and adorns it with every manner of veneration. He sees his primary task as keeping the body alive and preserving it at all cost. The end of the body is the end of the natural man.

It is no wonder that this natural man has painted his Creator in the same image and likeness as his perceived self and why he then fears this Creator of his own invention. Fear makes it crucially important to measure up to the strict guidelines of the ego god's judgment. To fail means to be inadequate and remain prisoner in some perceived state of eternal sorrow and to remain forever separated from our long-sought paradise. This has become such an obsession that through the ego identity we have made up stories to accommodate the judgmental forgiveness of all kinds of transgressions. This is sometimes achieved through some imagined third-party intermediary whom, according to the man-made stories that support it, remains above reproach and is above or divinely superior to the natural man. In one sense that is very true.

The "Spiritual Man" is very unlike the "natural man" in that, even though still seemingly present in the world of form, he does not see himself as separate and distinct from his environment. Spiritual Man does not entertain ideas of being separate from his seeming brothers and sisters or the rest of the universe, for that matter – he is "in the world, but not of the world". The Spiritual Man sees with Spiritual vision rather than with physical eyes only and because of this, the Spiritual Man sees beyond the current limited manifestations of universal law into their true essence. The Spiritual Man also sees his brothers and sisters as perfectly innocent and pure expressions of the same *essence* or Authentic Identity that is the origin of all there is in this perceived reality. He does not see through the eyes of guilt or blame, nor does he extract any sense of identity from any portion of the world of form.

Spiritual Man knows that there is no *real* existence on any *physical* level, and that the Spiritual connection to the Authentic Identity is the only voice of reason in this illusory world of form. This Man also understands that the five physical senses are inextricably linked to this framework of expression and experience. All that the senses can do is help to translate that which is illusion to that which is also illusion. If it can be experienced through the physical senses, it is the byproduct of a split mind; it is illusory. The five physical senses are constructs of the ego and only serve to reinforce the false sense of identity by reporting only that which supports and validates the illusion of its separate existence. Spiritual Man understands this universe's transitional nature, and makes no attachments to anything in the realm of perception. He maintains that nothing of value beyond the recognition of what we truly are can be extracted from this universe.

The natural man (ego identity) is but a superficial idea within an idea of the Spiritually connected Man (Authentic Identity) to which we have granted much power. However, no matter how dominant the ego nature may seem, there is always some inkling, a sort of peeking out of the Spiritual light, from beneath all of the egoic stories and subterfuge of the natural man that sees beyond the barriers put in place to obscure our memory of Truth. It is through misinterpreting these perfectly natural Spiritual experiences, these peekings-out, that many are further deceived. By our own devices, we accept further falsehoods as truths by fabricating more elaborate stories about the "supernatural" to support and validate these "natural" experiences of our own Spiritual presence. If one is not ready or willing to accept these experiences or glimpses beyond the veil of illusion as natural, they will often mistake them for something other than what they are. Some may invent stories that their mind is playing tricks on them or that they are losing their grip on the state they call sanity. Others may label these experiences as psychic or clairvoyant episodes brought on by any number of causes. Often these glimpses into the Authentic Identity will engender either fear or an illusion of even further specialness. All of this serving to set the perceived self apart from what appears to be others in order to classify ones self as "different" and "special".

I cannot stress this enough as it is the foundation of much of our misbelief. That is that the Truth needs no support, nor does it need us to believe it to remain the Truth. It is the lies and falsehoods that require our beliefs and stories in order to continue their existence. If there is a reflection of even a fragment of Truth within a falsehood or experience, the authentic part of us may sense its presence and be attracted to it. This is how so many are misled into proclaiming the illusory experience itself as the Truth. Some seekers succumb to the desire of the ego identity to remain special and independent from those perceived as having not yet discovered the pearl of wisdom hidden within the rubbish being handed out as salvation. They then pass themselves off as gurus of one sort or another. These gurus then continue the charade and play the role of spiritual leader and mystical teacher. They become the blind guides leading the blind followers.

The Spiritual Man has seen through the vicious cycle of birth and death and recognizes no need for the Earth-plane to express or experience real existence. Thus he sees well the opportunity to serve those seeming others that have chosen to remain in their limited individuality rather than investigate their attachment to the beliefs that block their realization of the Authentic Self. He helps those that wish help to awaken to the self that is no self yet is back of all selfness. This service is not supplied by shouting "Look at me, I've figured it all out and I alone can lead you out of your darkness." It is done by unconditional Love, perfect acceptance of what the seeming others perceive themselves to be – without judgment. Not to demand change or reformation, not to see some proverbial light, but to see the beauty that Spiritual light casts on every given moment. To Love what is, because it is a perfect opportunity to release the state of fractured and fragmented thought that maintains the illusion that fear built as we perceive it in this place of dreams and thoughts.

To know your brother is to know yourself, to gaze out into the cosmos and know that you are simply gazing into the memory of imaginary thoughts, is the beginning of wisdom. The natural man asserts that the "subjective mind" is some vastly greater portion of the mind and that it is hidden from us. In a very small sense, this is on the track of correctness. In human terms, the subjective mind is greater by comparison (if it were actually possible to separate and compare them), but by no means is it hidden from us. It is all around us constantly – it is our environment – it is the Universe. The natural man's fractured mind has separated itself from its environment and declared independent "selfhood", never the once realizing that it is impossible to conceive of anything without considering its containing environment as well.

The "objective mind" is the *perceived* self or the body, and the "subjective mind" is basically everything else, everything that is perceived as not self. The objective mind is only an aspect of the subjective mind "pretending" to recognize self as other than self. There is no "objective reality". There is only what appears to be the objectification of a subjective idea through the illusion of separation, which can never actually exist. The objective mind is just another thought within the thought.

At the level of form there is no power, because everything here is a reflection of what was. We see only the past in terms of what we experience as linear time. Natural man has agreed that the thought process that holds the universe in focused manifestation is far beyond his control. This universal thought process has been glorified and deified and looked upon as the creator. It is the one ego, Man's idea of man, which we have placed in the throne of power as a substitution for our relationship with Source. The natural man has agreed to believe that only the thought processes that occur at the body level are even marginally within mans control. Because of this agreement, man has placed himself into a victim role with regard to the rest of the universe. He has subsequently hidden deep within himself any awareness that he is able to transcend this illusion. When the natural man recognizes that his body as well as his environment (extended out to the universe and beyond) are products of the same illusion or dream state, he will then begin to realize that the Authentic Identity (or at least a tiny portion thereof) must be the Dreamer. He will then further realize that the perceived self in the realm of form is but a figment of the dream, not its creator. From this point, the perceived self, now beginning to "awaken" within the dream, can help the dream to heal the imagined idea of error which *is* the idea of separation.

Once again, we are confronted with questions that arise purely from the ego identity that beg to be answered concerning *personal power* in the world of form. That which is true and real knows no death and in any natural extension cannot act against itself lest all should surely perish and nothing would exist. Given this, any attempt to solicit the Authentic Self to alter the dream with the intentions of gaining power over another through the perceived "self" or "form" would simply be futile. False power is only an illusion within the illusion – a sort of exertion of some perceived will over the will of some seeming other. It remains only as long as the dominating will remains exerted and both parties agree to believe that the exerted will and its effects are in fact real. Therefore when I speak of false power, I refer to the sort of power that exists only within the ideas of form. Thus, false power is when one form exerts its will over that of another form.

The kind of power to which I just referred is that which one natural man may exert over another natural man through the medium of fear or the promise of reward. In such forms of false power, the seed of its own undoing is within the illusory nature of its presence. Authentic power does not come from the world of form and, therefore, anything expressed as power of one over another is merely the exertion of the will to control and is not "real" power. Any such control or power will immediately dissolve as soon as the dominating will is withdrawn. This is like redirecting the flow of water in a river by placing a large board in the stream and holding it there. As long as it is held in place by either the instigator or some means employed by the instigator, the water will be redirected. However, the instant that the board fails to remain in place for whatever reason, the flow of water will return to its own natural path.

As long as the natural man believes that he can die, the fear of death can be held over him and used to force his hand into servitude. Spiritual Man knows of no death and therefore cannot be coerced in such a manner as he places no *real* importance in the seeming existence of a body and knows that there is no "real" life therein. Spiritual Man allows nothing in the world of form to define him, for he knows that all structures are imaginary and will dissolve back into the nothingness from which they are imagined. The natural man clings to his every possession and sets in motion the machineries of defense to see that they remain protected. The presence of a defense strategy implies the belief in vulnerability. Therefore one who knows no vulnerability seeks no defense for they see nothing that needs defending.

Natural man judges wealth and success solely on the presence of these material and unstable things. Because of this, like the board in the river, if he fails to maintain and support this imaginary kingdom, it will return to its unmanaged state. It will return to the state spontaneously provided by nature – the dream untended. As long as these ideas within ideas (thought fragments that represent as individual selves or ego identities) agree there is death and that there must be competition for security, then there will be suffering and sorrow. For in the world of form, nothing can live unless something else dies (as perceived in form).

Through guilt and blame (which are actually one and the same) we perpetuate our fears of those things that remain unrecognized as us. Through guilt we place ourselves lower than the event or seeming other and accept that we are *deserving* of whatever misfortune we receive. It is through guilt that we believe that we are inadequate. Through blame, we place ourselves above the event or other and make *them* responsible for the current condition. So, it is through blame that we project the guilt we refuse to own onto seeming others and place them below us. Guilt is blame we assign to ourselves, and blame is guilt we assign to others. When at once we accept the path of unconditional Love as "Spiritual Man", we cease to see guilt or blame. Both are but illusory judgments supported only by an illusory separation. They are never real.

When we can see the Truth behind anything that does not appear to us as innocence, we can forgive our perceptions. That is, we come to recognize the perfect innocence in everything, rather than pardon that which we perceive as less than innocent. When we fail to recognize this innocence, we judge it according to our assessment of the perceived separation. This comes solely from comparing the current situation to our images of the past, there is no other way. When we fail to recognize our own peace, the only option is to judge something perceived as not self, and credit it with our current dissatisfaction in order to explain and justify the perceived absence of that peace. When we say: "forgive them for they know not what they do," we are not simply suggesting an ignorance of the universal law of cause and effect or in the expression of unconditional Love one to another. We are suggesting that these seeming

61

others actually believe that this dream within a dream *IS* the reality and that they do not as yet see, or readily accept, any reality beyond the one they experience with their five physical senses. Therefore, they truly do not know what they do even though, if asked, they are certain that they do know.

Forgiveness is never some magnanimous act of being the bigger person and pardoning some transgression perceived as having been committed by some lesser person. It is instead recognizing that within a dream nothing is real, and therefore nothing is really happening. By this, there is nothing that needs to be *excused* or *pardoned*, only recognized for what they really are. And what are they really? They are symbolic opportunities to recognize these false senses of self that we derive from our environment and its contents. The ego, by its very nature, is only present when we have extracted some imagined sense of self from these seeming others through our relationship with them. By imagining that our identity truly is to only know our self through what we are not then we become the product of judgment, and true forgiveness is impossible. However, once awakened to our true self, we see the face of Truth in everything that we gaze upon, and judgment becomes impossible, and true forgiveness becomes our natural state.

So, true forgiveness is to recognize the innocence in every seeming event and thing, rather than seeing only the constructions we have imposed upon them.

It is to recognize every brother and sister as your self and to accept that no transgression could have ever occurred. The judgmental form of forgiveness has been being practiced for thousands of years and we can all see just how well that has been working out. There are battles being fought on every continent and we are murdering each other off in ever increasing numbers. The only reason we see guilt in others is because we harbor it in ourselves. Until we are able to recognize our own innocence we will continue to punish everyone and everything. There is no escaping this. This will be discussed in more detail later on in this book. However, by understanding that everything, including what we perceive as self, is perfectly innocent and pure without blemish, we can break the grip that this viscous cycle that fear and guilt has us locked into.

• Chapter Five •

Authentic Identity and Mistaken Identity

•

I suppose the fist thing that we need to address here is the obvious – what is an identity? An identity is that which identifies *you* as delineated against all that is considered *not you*. Under this definition, the label "Authentic Identity" becomes somewhat of a misnomer. The Authentic Identity is in fact "no identity" at all, for in a perfect unity there is no sense of identity, not in any way *we* might think. So I will use this label for the expressed purpose of lending explanation to things that are abstract enough that they tend to defy any real explanation. That being said, I would have to stress the importance of any sense of identification that implies a multiplicity as being artificial or manufactured.

So why do I keep referring to the "Authentic Identity"? Because I am relating from a point of operation that is based on the idea of an independent ego (mistaken identity), that is why. From this point of view, I cannot communicate anything about the Authentic Identity (or anything about anything) without applying some sort of identifying label or symbol to it. As well, the symbols that I choose must be somewhat generally accepted at the very least. So, I hope you can imagine my dilemma as I try to explain the *real* from within a language that is, by its very definition, only fitted to describe the *unreal*. I have never let the impossible stop me before, and I have no intention of letting it stop me now. Another quick note, when I refer to the mind with a small "m", I am referring to what a human experiences as mind. I am referring to an imagined mind within an imagined mind.

If something can be named or described, we are talking about the conditioned rather than the absolute. As I have already discussed, everything within the framework of the conditioned is illusory and is only symbolic of something else. Even if that which it is symbolic of is yet another symbol of greater scope, it is still just a symbol. Eventually if we trace it back far enough, we come to a point where intellect and left-brained reasoning will afford us no further passage. We eventually come to a point of pure Spirit that links what really *is* to what is merely *experienced*. This Spirit connects the Authentic Identity to all of the imagined, mistaken identities. It connects the Dreamer with the dream. The ego based intellect simply cannot go there.

From the Spiritual standpoint, nothing is seen as holding a separate form for it knows only Perfect Oneness. There is no sway imposed by the opinions of duality, nor any of its trappings. Although the Spirit too is an artifact (it is the counterpart to the ego mind), the Spirit does not *need* the imagined mind to do what it does, whereas the imagined mind is a useless void without the Spirit. The Spirit is the active component in the thought process. The mind is the passive component in the thought process. It is the idea of a medium in which the thoughts become things by taking the impression of form. These impressions of form are the symbols that we interpret (perceive) as objects.

If something can be experienced or sensed through the ordinary senses, then it is fiction – it is illusion. Everything we experience through the ordinary senses is part of the mistaken identity. It is either, that which we label "self", our seeming physical presence, or that which we label "not self", our seeming environment extended to the outer reaches of the cosmos. Everything we call our "thinking" and everything we agree to in belief are also part of the mistaken identity by the symbols we attach to them and the labels by which we identify them. These symbols are all part of the imagined ego identity, and none of these will even approach an answer to this riddle we call our life and existence. If it helps you to save time, I'll tell you, the riddle has no solution. The belief that it does is just another level of control put in place by the idea of separation we experience as the ego identity. It's just more of the same – forever following an endless path that leads to nowhere.

Through the medium of consciousness and our ordinary "physical" senses we observe, what are essentially, a series of neutral mirrors (reflections) that make up our perceived environment. These mirrors only reflect back to us what a divided mind has set apart through projection, to show us where we perceive guilt or blame. They show us the places where we still extract some sense of "self-ness" separate from all else. From these reflections, we can translate the symbolic idea into a better understanding as to why we punish this imagined self. However, it will still be an ego-based interpretation of the Spiritual nature that is continuously nudging us to awaken. As we attempt to apply our labels to facilitate these explanations of our justification, we get ever further and further from our Spiritual nature and deeper and deeper into the imagined identity. We can either *be* it or *define* it; however, we cannot be and do both. For instance, we cannot *be* happy and *know* that we're happy at the same time. This is because in order to know that we are happy, we have to objectify the happiness to analyze and quantify it as something or some state we recognize as happiness. To objectify it we must define it as an object and in that moment, a sense of self appears to observe the object being defined. In this act, the two become separate objects – the self and the happiness. Thus, the happiness stops being what we *are* and starts being what we are *observing*.

Staying with the happiness analogy, often times what keeps us from being happy is the fact that we get locked into a loop of remembering a time when we *were* happy. We analyze how we felt then, and how we came to feel that way. Because we believe that outside conditions or events are responsible for our feelings about them, we question the ability of our current condition, circumstances or events to produce the same desired result. By comparing remembered happiness to the present state and qualifying its absence (or seeking to engineer its presence), we manage to keep happiness at a distance. If we simply release what we need happiness to mean to us and our images of it as a target or goal, we can release the blocks that we ourselves put in the way of being genuinely happy. We can't *make* ourselves happy, but we can *let* ourselves *be* happy. It seems that on some level, a level that we keep hidden from our awareness, we believe that we don't deserve happiness, or at least that it must come at some cost. This is also why we question happiness when it does happen. If we didn't question it, we would be happy all of the time, or more to the point, we wouldn't so consistently divert ourselves into unhappiness.

Behind the ego identity's left-brain analysis of the absolute, there lies an unarticulated knowing that stems from those "aha" moments where something becomes amazingly clear, while at the same time

69

remaining completely unexplainable. It is in this space of "knowing" that we extract an equally unarticulated understanding of that which pre-exists all knowing, all thinking and all believing. We sense the Authentic Identity, even if ever so slightly. Often times this experience is labeled as "seeing the light" or being "God-struck". Even experiencing the tiniest sliver of what is true and real in us can have a very profound effect on our perceptions and imaginings. As I stated earlier, the Authentic Identity is actually no identity at all, and this is more akin to what we experience at these "aha" moments – no identity. We experience a sense of clarity, as we are no longer the self that is having an experience. We *are* the experience and the awareness of it, all-in-one.

Many disciplines refer to this state as becoming selfless. Selflessness would, of course, imply having no ego identity at all. Being completely without ego thought in this illusory place is not really possible, but on a pragmatic level, we can accept that the ego is artificial and that any guidance or derision it provides us is artificial as well. Still the debate goes on with some saying that we need "more ego" and others saying we must eliminate the ego altogether. The fact of the matter is that as long as there is consciousness, there will be ego. The two are inextricably linked, one to the other, or more to the point, the two are one-and-the-same. So as long as we are operating within this illusory universe as projected sentient beings, we will be operating through the ego's interpretation of our being-ness. That is okay! The point is this: We would do quite well to release the ego as our guide and leader and recognize and utilize it as the tool of it's own undoing, and nothing more. Instead of clinging to some imagined uniqueness and standing witness to the validity of the ego thought system, we can surrender to our Spiritual nature and let the ego stand witness to the falseness of the ideas that support error.

When we listen to the guidance of the ego identity (mistaken identity), we are the blind follower being led by the blind guide. We are blind by choice, and we give over our control to a hazy reflection. This reflection is not even a good representation of Man's idea of man, let alone of Man. It is but a mere symbol we have substituted for what the imagination has imagined that a separate or individual self would be like. We blindly follow our mind anywhere it takes us, without question, even as it abuses us and tells us what failures we are or how inadequate we are.

The Authentic Identity does not produce this universe and its contents directly. The Authentic Identity simply had the idea of a thought – "what is a self?" My repeated references throughout this text of thoughts within thoughts within thoughts and ideas within ideas within ideas address this very point. That is to say, the IS extends the essence of Its being-ness or IS-ness. This IS-ness in like manner extends the essence of its being-ness. To use more common terms, God imagined Man, Man imagined man and man imagined universe. Thus, what we have been worshiping as "God", the creator of our universe, is in reality nothing more than the one ego identity that gives rise to the seeming multiplicity of ego identities.

What makes it even more difficult to recognize this is that we have imagined the ego as analytical, logical and, of course, quite persistent. We have it forever defining every phenomenon (reflection of the one idea of separation within itself) and attaching some idea of a separate self to every aspect of the reflection. It is these reflections or ideas that have been mistaken for individual "selves". This false self (ego), like a blind man throwing darts in a room full of dartboards, purely by the law of averages, will hit the bulls-eye or at least a score upon occasion. We then somehow manage to see this as the ego having a sense of knowing, intellect or cunning of its own. I assure you, it does not. However, these periodic successes of the logic patterns we have assigned to the ego, random as they may be, keep us hoping for better returns on our further invested devotion. This behavior continues even though the failures it produces vastly out-weigh all of its successes. What is even more ironic is that we then label this process "trial and error" and accept it as the "standard" process of what we perceive as progress or learning. We then agree to believe that we are achieving something of value.

The mistaken identity is of such a nature that there appears to be something lacking in it and that only through some means or some action outside of itself can this flaw or emptiness be remedied. It has no way of appearing otherwise, as it is operating through what is but a fragment of the whole consciousness. Therefore, it sees itself as separate and apart from all else that it perceives. If there is something that we must "become", "achieve" or "do" in order to be worthy of atonement, then that not only implies the *potential* for failure, but the *probability* of failure (if not the *absolute certainty* of it).

If this really were an either-or system, then religion's "all loving" God would necessarily be an "either-or" God. Any system that would proceed from an either-or God would thus be designed to embrace both success and failure, good and evil. Such a system would, by its inherent nature, tend to cancel itself out and produce nothing. This not only fails completely in producing unconditional Love, it fails to produce any real Love at all. The word that comes to me that seems to describe this best is "contempt". In my paradigm, unconditional Love and contempt are not synonymous. In my paradigm, we are absolutely innocent, perfect and whole, right now without the addition of outside applications. The Authentic Identity cannot be improved upon, nor can it be diminished in any way under any circumstances. That which is unreal can have no effect on that which is real. What we are is infinitely inclusive. We are first (and only) Effect of first (and only) Cause. Let there be no mistake about this.

• Chapter Six •

Life and Death
•

Our current beliefs systems have made us fear virtually everything in the world of form. At the top of the list, death presides as king over all of our fears. In this world, it is the death of the body, the death of a relationship, the death of a career, the death of *something* that feeds virtually all of our lesser fears. In the next world, it is the death of our soul or the eternal death of damnation for some imagined transgression that extends our fears beyond the grave. This fear pushes our earthly fears beyond the veil of the physical into the realm of the invisible and into what we believe is the unknowable. "Unknowable" is simply what we call our resistance to knowing. Nothing is unknowable; however, one thing is unknowable *while incarnate*. Only the absolute, the selfless infinite Oneness, is beyond our *complete* comprehension while in our current form. To completely know the absolute you must become the absolute, and you cannot do that from a point of operation (from the plane of the particular – the illusory universe of separate selves).

To release our fears is to dissolve the very foundation of our misery and release us from that which binds us to this experience. How then do we release our fears? First of all, every fear at its core, even the fear of death, is the belief in the idea that something we extract some portion of our identity from can be threatened or taken from us. Since nothing eternal can truly be threatened, our Authentic Identity is forever in a state of Grace. It is only those natures that are being imagined that, through our lack of understanding, we embrace as real that can ever be threatened. It is the mistaken identity that provides us with the images of loss and imminent suffering that spawns all of our fears both great and small.

The world of form is an experience where nothing can live unless something else dies. What we fear as death is but the dualistic counterpart to what we worship as life here in the physical world. Both are mechanical processes and thus, they are as well a part of the illusory stream of perception. Even though it cannot be seen or measured, we insist that men are killed, that they are cut down. Now is the death in the blade or is it in the man? Of course, it is seen as being in the man. Accordingly, we then only apply the word death to something that we believe has life. But does the body itself actually have life-in-itself? To that I say, "No, it does not." There is no life here in this false universe, only the *idea* of life, and the images that the mind holds up to validate this idea.

Life, as we perceive it here, is part of the illusion that contains it, and therefore not real. Not real like we think it is. Life, as we perceive it, has a conception, gestation and birth that all seemingly take place within a linear timeline in a relatively predictable pattern (mechanical process). At the point of birth, life as we know it has a beginning, a duration and culminates with death as an ending (again, mechanical process). If we agree that life extends beyond these parameters and that it simply enters into the equation at conception (or thereabouts), then what we are exists independently of this physical realm. If we are a presence without the body, then we are a presence without the body, *period*.

If this is the case, then what possible gain is there in entering into a physical form? If there is no alternative to entering physical form, then free will is a lie. However, if a mistaken identity sways us to accept this life as real and necessary, then all that is needed is to release this nature and the mistaken identity it holds as self. On the other hand, if there *is* something that we must become or accomplish by taking physical form, then we must accept that God has somehow fallen short in His creation. We must also accept that we possess the power to overrule God, and finish His incomplete work and change, fix or complete an inadequate creation. None of this could be further from the truth. We are whole and complete and perfect right now, not after some

77

imagined adjustment. There is nothing we need to accomplish, nor is there any possible improvement on what we already are that can be made from here. There is nothing that we can imagine doing here in this illusion, in this idea, that can have any effect on what we truly are.

If life as we perceive it is just another part of the illusion, then when we pass from the state we call living to the state we call dead, one of two things would happen. We will have released our attachment to the sense of self that we extract from illusions, and realizing that there is nothing here for us, we would awaken to the awareness of our Perfect Oneness. Or, we would go on believing that this universe is real and our participation is required in order to perfect it and keep our false identity intact. Or we may agree that it holds some mystery that we must in fact solve to gain access to paradise (or whatever it is we believe waits for us when we "make it"). In the first scenario, we come awake to the Authentic Identity, and the universe of form ceases to be external leaving us in our natural state of Perfect Oneness. In the second scenario, what it would seem we are experiencing is commonly referred to as reincarnation. We re-assume a human form and go through our same life all over again with new names, new faces and new settings. In this light, reincarnation could be viewed as repeating the same behavior while expecting different results. I have heard this explanation used many times as the fundamental description of insanity.

Therefore, in an over simplified explanation, if we are a presence without the body, then we will go on seeming to repeat scenario two for what will appear to us as thousands of lifetimes until we finally go through scenario one. The other over simplification to these scenarios is the scriptural explanation. Though we are a presence without the body, we live *once* and then pass into darkness, a non-state, after entering the state we call dead. We remain there until we are awakened from the darkness for the "judgment", and if found to be worthy of playing on God's team, we are then raised to some mystical place called Heaven where we spend eternity in happiness and bliss at Gods feet.

If, on the other hand, we are found unworthy of God's team, we are still awakened from the darkness, but instead of Heaven, we are awakened for damnation, to be sent to Hell – suffering unimaginable torment and torture for all eternity. The God I have been describing thus far is not a god at all. It is the ego identity that we have placed in the throne of power. Now this imagined identity filters and rules our experiences according to its own insane thought system of either-or thinking – according to duality. We grant this false identity authority to destroy anything that does not conform to serve the illusion of its continuation. We have made the ego idea lord and master over all that we perceive. We cannot serve two masters. By two masters I do not mean God and

Satan. In fact I am not referring to two entities at all. I am referring to the split mind divided within itself. So we either serve the Truth (unity, oneness, no divided mind) or we serve the illusion (duality, separation, multiply divided mind), for each requires the absence of the other. By absence here, I mean lack of recognition or expression, not vacancy.

If we are *not* a presence without the body, we must then agree that we enter into the equation somewhere between conception and first breath. We can agree that this takes place through whatever means that we hold to be true. Either through some biological act or through some sort of Divine intervention, whatever it is that represents as the "self" here on the earth plane, takes its place within, or attaches in some manner to the body. It matters little what we believe as to how this takes place. It matters only to the degree that it is helpful in understanding the true nature of our beliefs and how we make them real. The more we invest in falseness the more difficult it is to see beyond it.

However, in the scenario that we are *not* a presence without the body, what happens to us at death? At this point, are we but a glimmer, a figment in the Creators memory? Once again, does God then recreate us from memory, to reward or punish us according to our earthly performance? None of this suggests a loving or forgiving God either. In fact, quite to the contrary, it suggests a rather demanding, vengeful and hateful God. This is why I say that this is NOT God, but the ego we worship in place of Source. Also, the existence of "memory" suggests the existence of a past to be remembered. This would, by extension, imply a God that is bound by time. This, I assure you is not the case.

The ideas that we embrace about life, death and what waits for us after death, are all afflicted by the inverted nature of the ego thought system. In response to the fears held in place by the ego nature, the greater portion of consciousness places vital importance on the body and its continuation. The emotions place the importance on the seeming relations between bodies or persons (or things) and *their* continuation. Last but not least, there is always a tiny fragment of the mind that remembers the Spiritual Truth of ourselves and places the importance on *not* placing importance on anything in this universe. The Spiritual connection to our real nature is the only voice of reason in this insane dream, and it doesn't speak in a language that the ego can comprehend. In this place we lovingly call universe, our imagined existence is defined by the perceptions we hold of the dualistic systems that keep us a prisoner of their own maintenance. We have imagined the ego to take the form of a very believable illusion, and our attachment to the body is one that, at best, is extremely difficult to release so we strive to maintain it. As we release the ego's counsel and begin to release our unnatural attachment to the body, the ego thought system begins to flood the

81

mind with images of death, the king of all fears.

The body is nothing more than a projection of the ego mind and part of the dream/nightmare. Nothing about the body is life-in-itself and nothing about it is actually capable of sustaining a state describable as living. While that intangible thing that is "US" remains persistent in believing that this universe exists, we continue to be born into bodies that in turn, we believe must die. However, remove the veil, which is the "dream", that subdues the mind, and the true meaning of the universe is instantly revealed. Immediately, the Spiritual connection to the Authentic Self obtains to a reality beyond the restrictions of space and time in the Eternal Always. So surely the Life-In-Itself has nothing to do with the body or the universe. The illusion of life or livingness is supplied to the body or universe (the illusion) by the Authentic Self in the same way we (the imagined self) supply life to the players in our sleeping dreams within this waking dream.

Because man has accepted the idea that the body is real and has life, by extension he must also accept that it has death. Can this death be seen? No, it cannot. Therefore, it would appear that we are as well afraid of that which we cannot see or measure. We are afraid of everything that is connected with this universe, especially death. The idea that Man is made up of life and death is the fear that Life can be taken and replaced with death. If Life can be destroyed, then all is dead. However, if the illusion of death is dispelled, then there simply is no more death. We aren't here to keep this body alive. The body serves only as an instrument through which we can become present to certain aspects of our own nature that without it would not be possible.

From this line of reasoning, I have come to agree that nothing that is truly real can be genuinely threatened, and thus by extension, it becomes clear that nothing imagined or unreal can be genuinely threatening. The body, the environment, and even the entire Universe can be threatened, and as well destroyed, if given the right conditions and processes. Therefore, these things cannot be real in the absolute sense. Since nothing unreal can be a real threat, they cannot threaten us. At least not in the way that we currently believe they can – not in any *real* sense. Please keep in mind that *being* real and actually existing, as opposed to being *experienced* as real and actually existing are two completely unrelated ideas. Even though one seeming body can appear to threaten or destroy another, it has absolutely no effect on that which holds both bodies in focused manifestation. Nor has it any effect on the Authentic Identity.

Truth comes to us through our Spiritual nature to expose the unreality of this universe and the death it appears to wield through our fear. It comes to share the Absolute and the Eternal Always in True Light. The natural man teaches us that man must die; that both life and death make the man. Then where

83

exactly is "Man" in all of this? The universe illustrates man by various figures. To Wisdom, the Creator is the reality, and life and death are self-imposed conditions or ideas existing only within the illusion. The natural man makes himself a combination of life and death and when his life goes out, he is dead. Truth makes Spiritual Man as that which creates the light and darkness is the natural mans own impression. His light is his wisdom and his *wisdom* is his real life that is ONE with Source. Darkness is the belief in illusion, death and disease. As the light that Spiritual Man creates shines, it dispels the darkness of illusion and replaces thinking with knowing. This inner illumination is often referred to as Spiritual Vision.

Spiritual Man puts no life in the ideas of illusion and therefore his resurrection is from ignorance. The natural man's resurrection is from death because his substitute for wisdom still embraces it, and therefore his perceived wisdom will die with him. In all our teaching, Truth always strives to release falsehood. If we pretend to separate error from the truth by trying to give them various names like "good" and "evil", "right" and "wrong" or "life" and "death", etc., then these two "opposing" natures remain distinct and separate in the one man, just as night and day are included in one day. For to have any two distinct and separate natures, opposing or not, is to subscribe to the illusion of duality. The acceptance of duality is to validate the dream (nightmare) and agree that separation is real. Until we actually remove the perception based cause (belief in separation) the effect (the illusion and duality) will remain.

Life is not a thing, nor is it the state of a thing. Life is simply a label that consciousness places on those symbols that it accepts as being a part of the idea "alive". Unfortunately, consciousness is not a reliable source of information as to the nature of anything we experience because it is part of the illusion that it is experiencing. Therefore, it is bound by the same framework of limitation that binds this imagined universe. Consciousness is the operator of the ego thought system, and it seeks explanations through the physical senses and by seeking the counsel of its own reflections *of* itself *within* itself. The only thing that consciousness can report with any surety is information about the current state of the perceived duality. It is a closed loop that can only follow its own leadership. Any thing, or state of any thing, can only exist in a setting where its opposite can coexist with it – "life" and "death", "light" and "darkness" or "holy" and "evil". Therefore, there is no thing or state of a thing that is "life" there is only an idea that is called life. Our genuine nature has no opposite or counterpart, for it is all encompassing. Therefore it can neither be considered alive or dead. These ideas only have meaning to us here in the paradigm of separation.

Life and death are just another example of the mated pairs, polar opposites that make up these dualistic geometries of the ego thought system. All of these seeming thought geometries have been evolved by the consciousness within the seeming process of explaining the idea *of* the imaginary self *to* the imaginary self. Life is only life when there is a perceived belief in death. When we remove the possibility of death, there is only an "IS-ness"; no birth, no life, no death, just "IS". Life and death are simply labels that have been applied by consciousness to symbols that are agreed upon as being of that kind of object, or state of an object, as represented or described as being "alive". The active (or animated) are generally accepted as being "alive" and the passive (or inanimate) are considered as "dead". The underlying essence, or that which is back of the experience, never changes in either case. Only the modes of expression that are experienced by the objective faculties appear to go through any transition, or maintain one or the other state.

So it would seem that we imagine everything that we perceive as "alive" through a combination or mixture of both life and death. We judge our preferences depending upon the polar extreme to which they draw nearest. We see a newborn baby as being a combination of mostly life and very little death. Therefore, we covet and cherish and protect this form above many others. These are considered as very attractive to us. As the same seeming individual approaches the end point in its normal life expectancy, we see them as being a combination of mostly death and very little life. This condition is not as attractive to us so we tend to resist such situations. Where caring for an infant at every moment and changing its diapers is considered a normal and perfectly accepted routine, caring for the elderly at every moment and changing their diapers is too often considered to be more of a burden.

I am not saying that we do not love our elderly; only that our fears make them unattractive to us. Their nearing mortality engenders the fear of our own death. We would rather remember them in some past form as healthy and vital rather than sickly and dying. This is because the ego thought system holds to the belief that although the body must age, decay and die, it can "hide" from death until the last possible moment. The belief is that life can be had without death, simply by avoiding or denying anything associated with death, has never worked. Yet this idea is exemplary of the delusional nature of the ego thought system. The ego thought system cannot see beyond the illusion, and as well is certain that it, the ego, is the only expressed power within the illusion. The life of the ego begins with birth (or thereabouts) and ends with death. This is why, as seeming humans, we tend to fear death so much, because to the ego it symbolizes the end. The ego's entire being-ness is bound to the sense of "self" that only exists as a product of relationship with that which is considered as "not self" and is inextricably linked to these points of operation, these bodies.

The ego covets and worships the body as its temple and even though in some cases appears to abuse it horribly, it still exalts it as its only refuge from the darkness that it thinks it is escaping by imagining itself [ego] as the light. Even though the only light that it knows is perceived light, it still cannot free itself from the fact that it is only an idea within an idea. In-and-of-itself the ego is nothing and having no real causative power of its own, the only light it can ever know will be imagined or dreamed. Without any admission, the ego knows that it is always "living" at the expense of another, or so it believes. The gain of one is always the sacrifice of another.

It is from the initial idea of ego that the idea of multiple experiences of *"self and other"* arises. It is also from the ego's believed powers of self-deduction that we harbor our guilt and shame, stemming from the very idea of the life we believe we are living. It is because the underlying absolute that gives rise to us all, knows that the Creator and Creation are a Perfect Oneness and that this can never be otherwise. The ego believes that through the very fabrication of its perceived "selves", the Perfect Oneness has been destroyed and replaced with a multiplicity. The ego-distorted belief is that it has undone the very foundations of creation. It holds the idea that it has replaced the Oneness and diminished the Creator and the Creation, and made each one vulnerable. It believes that it has usurped the Creator's power and now places itself in the seat of power (imagined light rather than the true living light). Under any circumstance, this is completely impossible. However, as I stated before, the ego's thought system is purely delusional.

I hope that you can now see that the ego identity is a manufactured idea, an illusion. It has, in turn, manufactured the idea of "life" as a testimonial to its power, which is also illusory – ideas within ideas within ideas. Since the ego is a product of the idea of separation (as is everything in this thought system, this universe), it can only perceive in terms of duality and multiplicity. Therefore, as it imagined the idea of life, it also imagined the idea of death. This is unavoidable within a duality, as you cannot have any one thing (idea) without its accompanying opposite. There cannot be a thing (idea) that is accepted as life unless there is as well a thing (idea) that is accepted as *not* life. Please keep in mind that all of these things (ideas) are illusions – they are temporary things we call life and death. Since that which we call life in this illusory universe can be threatened, it cannot be genuinely real.

From this false seat of power the ego has proclaimed itself "lord and creator" of this imagined universe and all of the imagined life therein. The ego casts the illusion that it gives life so it can threaten this life with death to maintain its false kingdom through fear. When at once we recognize the falseness and unreality of this wholly illusory position of authority, we can liberate our seeming selves from the role of the blind followers of the blind guide. We can release our imagined need to seek endlessly down the illusory path of life that leads only to sure death – over and over again.

• Chapter Seven •

Thinking, Believing and Knowing

•

The sensations we perceive in our awareness, that we agree to call our "thoughts", are but fragments – reflections of an "idea" of complete knowing viewed through the filter of separation. Not fragments in the sense that the complete knowing has been shattered or divided, but rather, fragments in the sense that the idea of separation has produced a consciousness unsuited to the task of simultaneous collective awareness. It has become the seemingly numberless pinpoints of observation within the "infinity" that our consciousness *pretends* to represent. This is because as seeming individuals we only possess a "pinpoint" perspective of what we can only imagine as infinity. The vast majority of knowing either remains enshrouded in mystery, or remains unseen altogether. This mystery is the source of all of our beliefs (stories), because the ego identity is not capable of filling in the gaps as it has NO knowing in-and-of-itself. As such, under the ego's guidance, we fabricate believable untruths to bridge the gap and resolve the seeming discrepancies in continuity, for the only thing the ego identity seeks is continuity.

That which we call human thinking is not thinking at all. It is nothing more than the fragmented parade of images that the ego mind has put to ego level interpretations. It is but a dialog about the past conducted within the various natures of the fabricated self. It is essentially the narration of the ego's *story* of thinking. It all occurs in what we, as humans, would call the past. It would appear that as humans we don't actually tend to employ *real* thinking. Real thinking is a "spatial experience", not a "linear process". Real thinking (as real as it gets for us) is an all-inclusive experience occurring simultaneously in the ever present "now" and is often misinterpreted as a religious or mystical experience and becomes distorted into something that it is not. That is to say that it isn't the product of a sequence of thoughts or thought segments that ultimately lead to some sort of imagined conclusion. There are no real conclusions. The expression of linear human thinking is what could be referred to as deductive reasoning, or more accurately, a deductive analysis of the past. Thinking of this type and nature is traditionally considered to be a product of the subjective influences on the objective mind. The classic syllogism, if A is true and B is true, then C can be inferred as true. However, this only leads us further into a belief structure that validates the reality of the illusion. If we accept that either premise A or B are real, then the framework of perception that contains them must as well be real. In this manner human thinking stands as testimonial to validate the false thought system and false reality of the imagined separate self and its relationship with the thinking that holds it captive in its own images.

The thinking associated with the ego identity is always a linear process, an illusion that is both fashioned and bound by the same constraints as are space and time. We use words such as "thinking" and "idea" to describe ego states of illusory progression, and as the indisputable evidence of our individual uniqueness. We tend to separate one from another by the contents of their "thoughts" as though they were somehow local to the seeming individual who claims them as their own. Words like "thought" and "idea" have no meaning in the absolute. Only here in the realm of the conditioned illusory universe do they take on any meaning. This is because we even separate our *selves* from our *thoughts*. We refer to them as "my" thoughts and "your" thoughts as if they were possessions.

What we accept as human thinking is nothing more than, for lack of a better description, residual echoes of the ego identity's continuous fragmenting of the original idea of a self into numberless bits. Human reasoning is little more than the geometries of perception that go into the accounting for the description of these bits as individual objects. The ego thought system ceaselessly arranges and rearranges these seeming bits and pretends through each of the imagined iterations that something new is being created. It then holds these up as proof of its inherent power to create. The ego is not capable of creating anything new – ever. Nothing new is ever possible because within the infinite, all possibilities already and always exist lest it would not be "infinite".

As long as we accept the perceived workings of our assumed brain as real thinking, we will not be able to release the mistaken identity or understand our Authentic Identity. The Absolute can only be realized by releasing the imagined self and the so-called *thinking* it employs and to *allow* the infinite to reveal through us. We cannot *make* it happen; we can only *let* it happen. Or more to the point, stop preventing it from happening. As long as the "self" is present, the Absolute is not. Seeking through any means, be it thought, the intellect or even consciousness, will never yield any *real* results. To *seek* in any fashion, by definition, is to accept the belief that there is something – anything – that is separate and apart from us that must be located and claimed or reclaimed. This is simply not possible. In the absolute there is nothing that is separate or apart from us that must be sought. It is only within the idea of a self that anything can appear to have an existence separate and apart from anything else.

What we call human thought always leads to more human thought and never to an actual resolution. This is because, like the ego at the source of it, it can never be complete. It can never answer anything, it can only question it as it has only itself for counsel. Every question leads not to an answer but only to more questions. It is a relentless unquenchable cycle that will keep us distracted from ever meditating on the present moment. The reason we so often fail to see this is because we are asking the source of the problem to help free us from the problem that it is creating by its very existence. We are asking the riddle for its own solution. If you don't believe me, consider this: What is the first thing we do when we discover that our thoughts are troubling us? We sit and think about it. We ask our thoughts about our troubled thoughts to free us from our troubling thoughts.

If we wish to seek, seek we will. However, it is not by seeking that we shall find, but by realizing that there is nothing to seek, for we already possess everything. We need only learn to recognize our wealth. The mind, the ego, the consciousness and human thinking are all part of the illusion. They all set us into imaginary motion solving some imaginary riddle that will set us free and get us home. As long as we serve them, we will never see that they only keep us from being present to the moment, from being still and realizing that we are already home. Not home here in the world of form, but home in our

True nature with Source, the "IS", in the Eternal Always. We have never, in fact, left home, only in the *idea* of a thought. That is to say – not human thought; real thought. However, having no capacity for real thought, we (the ego identity) refuse to accept this as so, *and* that this riddle we seek, cannot be solved. We are certain that if we are diligent in our efforts and remain persistent in our beliefs, we will at some point succeed in solving the meaningless riddle of life. The ego denies that it can ever be wrong.

That is enough about human *thinking* for now. Let's move on to our knack for *believing* what we think. As I stated earlier, thought is a closed loop which would make our beliefs captive of our thought system with nowhere to go. We say that we believe in so many things, however, we tend to only *realize* our beliefs in those things that we perceive as essentially positive or personally defining – things we would care to carry in conversation. What we fail to see is that we accept into belief many things that we have no need of, or any good use for. For instance, we may admit belief in some sort of Divine Creator, in Love and Truth, and the inherent good of mankind. We may admit to all of these while at the same time ignoring that we have also accepted beliefs in separation, sickness, disease, violence, hatred, war and death. We accept the latter simply because they have been accepted by those whom have gone before and since we are trained by these previous humans, we unconsciously condition our fabricated identity to accept them as a matter of course.

Even though we may not embrace the latter or express them in our seeming daily lives on the behavioral level, we have agreed to believe in them nonetheless. Only through our ongoing belief in them do they take their existence in this world of form, as they have no causative source in themselves. They cannot live without us. I want to impress upon you that if left unto their selves and unchecked by the "knowing" in you that is the Spiritual connection to Truth, your beliefs will cause you more misery than joy in the long run. You may say that your positive beliefs bring you comfort in times of misery or tragedy. In this dualistic universe, every seeming positive belief automatically has its matching negative belief. It is the resistance to these negative beliefs that bring you those moments of misery and tragedy in the first place. You may say that this is my opinion, and you would be accurate in your assessment. Unless, of course, I can manage to appeal to that place of knowing within the point of operation you see as your "self", and persuade.

Let me then try to explain – You say that you believe in all of these positive things and many more of the like. You feel that these beliefs give what you call your life a richer more fulfilling meaning. However, every time there is evidence to the contrary or there are symptoms that contradict one or more of your beliefs, it often engenders doubt and/or fear. Any doubt or fear can and will undermine your beliefs and often lead you to alter or replace them, thus never allowing stability. Where there is fear there can not be Love, the two are mutually exclusive. This will have a hobbling effect on your inner peace and outer harmonious existence as it is not possible to be happy and afraid at the same time. It does this by keeping you in, what is at best, a marginalized state balancing these anxieties and fears. This in turn will keep you from being present to the moment where you can examine the source and foundation of these beliefs, and what it is we are attaching them to, as they are brought to bear. You will be too busy suffering the past and fearing the future as you race about shoring up the crumbling walls of your belief structure and erecting the replacement walls for the ones that have failed you already.

There can be no genuine peace where there is doubt or fear, and there is no doubt or fear where there is the "knowing" through the Spirit. Therefore, it is not what we believe that brings us peace; it is what we "know" through the presence of the Spirit that makes for a genuine livable peace. The ego pushes its linear thinking and its linear beliefs, but the ego can never know the Truth. The ego can never really know because the ego is not real and thus can never *know* the Spirit. These two are mutually exclusive as well. Where the ego is recognized the Spirit is not heard. Where the Spirit is recognized, the ego cannot go.

So you see, if there is naught except for the Creator, and the Creator simply IS, then how anything that is not of the Creator can have any real existence in itself becomes clearly impossible. There cannot be two infinities as each one would limit the other, nor can there be a duality as each opposite would cancel out the other and would result in a stalemate. Not to mention that any form of duality precludes any infinitude. Therefore, only within the seeming individual mind, the ego identity, can the belief in that which is contrary to Truth or Love be given any existence. This existence then is wholly contingent upon the continued maintenance of these wrongful beliefs held as truth within the seeming individuals or ego identities. Therefore, under the guidance of the ego identity, we are the sole source of their manifestation and continuity.

Through the ego identity we engender within our imagined selves, human thoughts that the seeming self is comprised only of the traits that the same self sees as "agreeable". By these same means, we suggest to our imagined selves that all of the other traits, the "disagreeable" traits, exist out there, in others. This leaves the impression that these traits are separate and apart from the seeming *self*. This way each of us can see ourselves as superior and justified as we project blame onto those others. The idea of *self* resists any qualities that it deems undesirable, thus projecting them into what is experienced as an outside world. This is where phrases like "resist not evil", and "love thine enemy" originate. For that which we hate, reject, resist or deny will find their outlet in ways the *self* will perceive as *elsewhere*. When we come to recognize this about ourselves, we will be free of the states that these qualities engender when we attach to them and the suffering they inevitably bring to our door. To "resist not evil" does not mean to join in and participate in committing evil. It means do not give over your power to any negative state by engaging it in conflict and opposition.

In order to have an enemy, we must first be an enemy. This is because hate, rejection and denial all originate in the same place that the idea of an enemy originates. They originate in the ego identity, and nowhere else. As I stated earlier, we cannot imagine a positive without simultaneously invoking its opposite. The moment we say something is "good" we must also include that which is perceived as "bad". Resistance and rejection of what we perceive as "undesirable" won't prevent any of these traits from expressing. It only prevents the seeming self from recognizing the truth of their falseness and the emptiness of their expression. This is because they appear ever so real once projected.

So, upon looking outside of our seeming selves at what appears to be a vastly diverse, complex and chaotic world, what is it we are actually looking at? The fact of the matter is that we have no idea what we are looking at. We only know what we perceive, and perception is purely an illusion occurring entirely within what we call a human mind. We are looking at what can best be described as our group or collective (human) thoughts being projected onto a neutral medium that only shows us what we are holding as truth at any given moment. This is why we see so much chaos, violence and separation of people, countries and beliefs. The guilt we harbor against ourselves is the same guilt we project onto others to hold them responsible for all we perceive as wrong or needing correction. Through this guilt we believe that punishment is not only deserved, but mandatory. It is for the sake of our false beliefs that we hold to be the truth that we continue to subject ourselves to this nightmare (illusion).

The Truth exists whether we believe in it or not. It is only the deception or illusion that requires our beliefs to maintain its existence. Without belief to support it, the illusion simply vanishes as would the ego, for these are but fabrications of the mind, having no Truth in them. That which is of the Truth is singular in nature and therefore cannot act against itself lest all should perish. That which seems to act against the Truth is simply the absence of Truth and is nothing more than a "belief in error" attempting to return to Truth. One should never endeavor to believe that which is not true, nor ever embrace falsity because it is handed down to you from one boldly proclaiming it as Truth. Ultimately, it always comes back to the guide whose counsel you choose to follow that decides what is accepted into belief and embraced as that which defines. Do you listen to the worldly guide (ego – the closed system having only itself fro counsel) or the Spiritual guide (our limitless true nature needing no counsel)?

A belief is one thing, while the thing that is believed is quite another. Our happiness or misery is only our ego identity's belief, and the things believed have neither happiness nor misery in them. Now it is of vast importance to know what it is we believe and why we believe it – for that which we *know* we have no belief of, we have proof. As such, it is that which we do *not know* which remains a mystery and causes us to create all manner of belief. A belief is nothing more than a story that we agree to accept as the explanation for something that, without which, there is currently no explanation. This is where we can exercise caution, in the beliefs that we accept or reject based upon some self-accredited *judgment*. When we are convinced of the truthfulness of any belief and we accept it into our imagined pool of "intellectual wisdom", universal laws and forces are set immediately into action to supply these beliefs with form and evidence (or symptoms) of their apparent real existence. All beliefs take their existence in the vain imaginings of the ego identity.

In the cases where a belief does not spontaneously evoke a disharmonious state, there may well be a deeper truth behind the belief that is being symbolically delivered through a sort of Spiritual counsel. An example of such a belief could be "kindness is its own reward". In these cases favorable conditions and experiences may be brought forth. However, where a belief is founded in error or opinion brought to us through ego's counsel, the opposite is the generally case. From this, all misery and undesirable conditions arise. An example of such a belief could be "When I get that promotion, I will be happy." What we call happiness and misery are the *effects* of our beliefs as we put them in practice.

Any belief that we hold true that can bind burden or hardship to another also binds it to us. To believe that anyone can have any irregularity or disease or anything of the sort (even if we believe ourselves to be free of such) will always subject ourselves to the same. It is not the belief that *anyone else* may become afflicted, it is the belief that *anyone at all* may become afflicted – which will always include ourselves, as we are all ONE. We can learn to see the perfection that is in all, through all and above all.

We cannot rely on mere belief to bridge the gap between suffering and peace. We might initially accept some things on belief, but we can captivate each belief and inspect it. We can look for the correlative Truth that rises from the Spiritual nature within each of us that gives vitality and substance to any of these seeming external beliefs. We must prove them to be of that Oneness that pre-exists all belief and then quit *believing* and start *knowing*. It is *revelation* that has shown them to us and made their meaning *known* to us. If you cannot find such a correlative Truth within yourself, then you must accept that the belief is in error and discard it no matter how attractive it appears to you on the surface.

That which is Truth cannot be threatened, destroyed, changed or deceived. Truth is absolute and is the same no matter the direction from which you approach it. Belief, on the other hand, is uncertain and subject to change, reformation and even abandonment. In the face of conflicting evidence or a persuasive alternate belief it is often easier to redefine (adjust) the belief than it is to justify the need to keep it in its current state. Or we go to war to protect or defend some beliefs and resist outside influences that threaten other beliefs.

That which is false has no source in itself and thus possesses within its own nature the foundation of its own undoing. Only that which is *true* is eternal and remains the same through all experience. A belief is like reading a book about doing something (a linear logical process) – the knowing of the Spirit is like actually doing the thing (a spatial experience). So, I repeat, the Truth exists whether we believe in it or not, it is that which is not of the truth that requires our belief in it to exist at all. The falseness cannot hold on to us. It is we that hold on to the falseness.

Let's take a look at another aspect of belief, the idea of "faith". In my understanding, the word faith has been somewhat mixed up with the words "belief" and "trust". Faith is not a noun, faith is a verb – it is not the belief one holds about something, but the action one takes based on their beliefs. This action either transforms the darkness of these beliefs into the light of knowing, or it dismisses them as the vain imaginings of the ego thought system. Faith is not the *belief* that you can walk on water. Faith is *stepping* out of the boat. Faith occurs when we *know* that the Truth is what we *are* and therefore can never act against us.

Faith as simple belief becomes just another word in the dictionary; faith as action becomes Truth expressed as wisdom. I use a small "w" for wisdom here to represent "human wisdom". By human wisdom, as I use it here, I do not mean catchy slogans or quotable quotes. I mean a presence of being-ness that connects with the Authentic Identity and transcends this world of form. The Truth is far too vast to express in this imagined place, but more to the point, if Truth *were* able to present in this place, it would make real this unreality. This, can and will, never happen. Because that which is unreal can never be raised to the real, and that which is real can never be reduced to the unreal.

Our attachment to the trinkets and bobbles of our imagination is what keeps us *believing* in the illusion that is our present life. Our unquestioned affinity for the unreal is what keeps us from recognizing its unreality. All of this pledges service to the idea of faith as belief or trust. We often buy into things or ideas that we have no need for simply because they are offered to us in a state of trust. By this I mean that the one whom offers the thing or idea is one whom we trust for one reason or another. They may be a parent, doctor, clergy, teacher or a person of some social esteem, or whatever sort of person we see as being inherently trustworthy. Without question, we sometimes allow their wares to become our wares. However, there is always a price attached and when it comes time to pay we may find that the cost is more than we have to justify this thing or idea that we had no real need of in the first place.

Now we are cast into a sort of prison for this Spiritual debt. It is a prison where the bars are the false beliefs that we have accepted. That is to say, this idea or thing binds us down like a tether or chain. Sometimes we are completely unaware of the source of this binding or even that we are bound at all, but we remain bound nonetheless. The Truth comes to us and shows us the error of our acquisition and frees us from our debt which is our false belief, and as a result we are at once put at liberty. This Truth makes these things clear to our understanding, which then allows us to *know* how to distinguish between "error" and "Truth". The useless belief, which is the error or ignorance of the world, is the acquisition which has put us in debt, and by not recognizing the error, has resulted in our bondage. The Truth of our Divine nature is our riches and as such frees us from our assumed Spiritual debt. Those whom we trusted without question are the peddlers who provided us the false ideas that bound us down in the first place. Often times these ideas are delivered absent of any malice or intent to deceive. Sometimes these ideas are simply the best that the "peddler" had to offer at that time.

Before we buy into any idea, we can first find the correlative Truth that is always there within us. That Spiritual connection to our Authentic Self that rings from absolute Truth, and senses the nature of the thing or idea and makes the idea's *true* nature *known* to us. If there is no interior sense of the thing or idea, and only exterior support for its seeming presence, then it is the ego identity that seduces us into claiming it as real. If we *do* find the correlative Truth within ourselves, then we will find it to be of that which is True and Real, and we will see that it was symbolically relayed to us (ego identity) through our Spiritual identity. Then we *know* that it represents or reflects something that is real and eternal and that it will not bind us down but only lift us upward in its wisdom or Spirit toward the memory of our True nature. We then have a *knowing* of the thing or idea, and therefore, of it we need no belief, as we now *know* it to be a genuine presence within us. I might be going out on a limb here, but nothing that we are able to experience with the five physical senses falls fully into the category of the real. Everything that we believe we "know" about this place is fiction. Why not? It is only fitting since we have confused map with territory, information with knowledge, education with intelligence, thought with thinker, and too many more to continue.

We can choose not to abide in the uncertain world of "mystery" or "hazy beliefs" where superstitions are born. Such places are inherently unstable and will eventually consume themselves. We instead can choose to live in the world of Truth as revealed by Spirit, and through the sure knowledge and proof that its foundations extend firmly from the Love, which is of the Source, is thereby eternal. Remember always as you make your way, that everyone is your teacher and everyone is your pupil. Most importantly, be ever so clear that every lesson you both give and receive is of the Truth – that they have their essence in the Wisdom or Spirit – connected to the Authentic Identity. There is nothing that can be "gained" from the imaginations imagination that only "dreams" of the ego identity. There is nothing that can be "gained" at all.

This is not to say that all belief is wrong or in error. Even the mighty oak starts as but a small acorn which contains within it all that is necessary to bring forth the tree. Certainly the belief, like the seed that is rooted in Peace and nourished by Spirit, will never bind us down. However, do not remain content to preserve any belief on that shelf undisputed. All human knowledge starts out as an external belief, but we must still take it and prove it within. Once proven, we can live it in the sureness of its authenticity without fear. Then when we teach it, we can do so with the peaceful loving confidence that only Wisdom or Spirit can bring forth as an extension of the Authenticity it represents. Also, we can rest assured that our every pupil will be raised by it as well.

You will *know* that each ear upon which it falls will be enriched and increased in the same wisdom that allows the universe to be held in focused manifestation and all the seeming life therein – our Authentic Identity. Remember, that which is true can never be threatened or destroyed, and that which is error can never sustain. For every Truth that is present in the Absolute, there is a correlative Truth available to each seeming Individual through counsel of the Spirit. Once the "Believer" becomes the "Knower", a very important step has been made in the transformation process of releasing the ego guidance and embracing the Spirit's Knowing, for in the Knower resides the absolute surety of the oneness of all that is. In this absolute knowledge, you can then prepare for the step from *knowing* to *being*.

• Chapter Eight •

Forgiveness and Peace

•

How many times have you heard it said that we should "be the bigger person and forgive" or "forgive and forget"? These statements are very curious indeed. Yet they are the backbone of our generally held ideas about forgiveness. Through this widely held paradigm, it is implied that there *is* in fact something that actually *needs* to be pardoned through *our forgiveness.* It also implies that, through some magnanimous act of selflessness, this event is as well in need of *forgetting.* On the surface, this form of forgiveness seems like the thing to do when confronted with circumstances or events that we perceive as objectionable. The underlying messages, however, are and have been routing us into multiple layers of dualistic thinking that will actually draw us deeper into the ego identity's idea of peace through power rather than any real forgiveness. The ego's dualistic idea of forgiveness will never offer the peace that *true* recognition of the moment can and will provide.

Instead of peace, the ego's thought system can only provide for a stand-off experience that involves a perpetrator–victim type model. This is true even if what is being perpetrated is an act of kindness and the victim is seemingly a victim of enjoyment. So as you can see, even our seeming "good deeds" are as much of a worldly distraction as are our seeming "atrocities". This is not to say that we not concern ourselves with the nature or content of our actions, but that we would do well to release the need to fulfill any personal or worldly needs through our actions. That is to say, release the need to extract any sense of local or global identity from anything we encounter. From this, it is obvious that our acts of kindness rather than hostility make for a much more pleasant experience during our stay here in this imaginary place of our own making. However, if we attach meaning and value to the outcome of any of our actions, we are deceiving ourselves into accepting the unreal as the real and giving ourselves over to it.

So whether we experience it through a sense of gratitude of benefit or forgiveness of transgression, the process is still the same. You are making the external "something" real by recognizing it as a target for the emotion or action you deem appropriate as a response (or reaction) to it. In gratitude, you make yourself smaller than the "something" and attempt to rise to a state of worthiness of it. In judgmental forgiveness, you make yourself larger than the event and attempt to raise the seeming "something" to a worthiness of you. Either way, the ego's thought system is imagining a distinction between that which is considered as "self" and that which is considered as "not self" and judges the relationship between the two. In this system, the ego nature arranges the foundation and framework that will house the seeming elements of conflict that outward appearances seem to support. Whether the outward appearance of some imagined conflict is benign or hostile, the inner workings are the same. Each seeming player is attempting to gain something they perceive they lack, or something perceived as having value, from the seeming other. Or, we are attempting to defend ourselves or the things we see as having value from the poaching of another. The ego cannot meet any of its own needs; therefore, the ego must look outside itself to that which it perceives as being able to meet those needs. The ego cannot know itself except through its relationships with that which it sees as not self.

By our traditional concept of forgiveness, we are creating several roadblocks to our genuine sense of freedom and peace, let alone any forgiveness itself. The first block we set up is in believing that there is something that actually happened outside of us, and that it needs to be pardoned. We then continue on an unconscious level to accept that the players themselves actually exist in a capacity that can inflict such a transgression one upon the other. By

113

accepting this, we also must accept into concrete reality the existence of the environment in which the players are playing: the container, so-to-speak. Next, we compound this with the necessity to agree that the "transgression" is also an absolute reality and as well that the act of "forgiving" or "pardoning" it is also real, not to mention necessary. This is all according to our apprehension of the seeming event. All of these things exist only in the idea of duality, a state which by its very nature cannot exist in a perfect unity. It is only through a mind divided within itself that separation and conflict can be experienced at all.

The traditional concept of forgiveness is a completely egocentric mechanism wherein one puts their seeming self above some other first through the condemning and then the forgiving act. We even call it, "being the bigger person". This generally accepted idea of forgiveness requires that one party be "wrong" so that the other party, the forgiving party, can be "right". This is because we, as egocentric humans, tend to be of an "either–or" mentality. If it isn't black then it must be white; if it isn't right then it must be wrong. These are all parts of the false identity's process of separation and labeling. It is the ego identity that must be "right"; it is the ego identity that must assert itself. We eventually come to understand that there is no right and wrong, no good and evil, no light and dark. These are all simply ideas into which the ego identity has suspended yet another idea – the idea of a self.

The Authentic nature does not put any weight on ideas like "right" and "wrong" or "good" and "evil" because neither it, nor our Spiritual connection to it, subscribes to the idea of separation and duality. The Spirit abides only as the connection between the seeming dream of separation and the Dreamer which remains in Perfect Oneness. Therefore, it is impossible to separate "things" and compare one thing with another if there is only a Perfect Oneness. It is only in the idea of a thought within a thought within a thought that we imagine this illusory premise to be real. The "thought within a thought ..." is only an analogy and not an accurate description. It is but a metaphor to invoke a certain kind of mental image and in no way even comes close to describing the dream state, the Dreamer, the dream within a dream within a dream, or thought within a thought within a thought. It only serves as a vehicle through which I am attempting to communicate the nature of this abstraction.

True forgiveness is not any sort of pardon. It is an acknowledgement of the illusory nature of this experience in that it is not some world inflicting something upon us, but merely one mode of expression revealing to us that which at present remains enshrouded in darkness. It is the acceptance that nothing at all has ever actually happened as we would have ourselves believe. Thus, true forgiveness is the recognition of the pure innocence not only in ourselves, but also in every one of our seeming brothers and sisters, and by brothers and sisters I don't mean just people. I mean everything. So, just as it is in your sleep when you enter yet another layer of dreaming within the dream, if you see someone you think you know and they commit some act against you, you do not seek them out in the morning to extract retribution. You do not because in these cases, after you have awakened, you know that it was just a dream and that none of the seeming acts actually occurred. So it is in our waking dream as well. When we awaken from our waking dream, we will see that what we have accepted through perception hasn't really happened at all.

Even though while we are sleeping we are unaware that we are dreaming at the time, as it often seems very real. It isn't until we awaken from our dream that we realize that we were, in fact, just dreaming. It is the same within this larger dream within the dream. We do not realize that it is not real, not the way we think it is, and that it only exists as a thought, or more literally the idea of a thought, and nowhere else. The more and more we come to understand the purely subjective nature of our experiences, the more we are able to release the grip that we appear compelled to hold on them. Subsequently, this release frees us from the tormenting we invoke within ourselves at the behest of these ego level illusions.

The only way that we can find peace *without* is to make peace *within*. As well, the only way we can have an enemy without is if we are an enemy within. What we experience as the seeming world around us is but a projection of that which we judge or embrace within. So to find real lasting peace, we must first forgive the enemies we battle within. The only way we can accomplish this is to forgive the enemies we perceive without and acknowledge that they, as well as our perceived self, are only thoughts within thoughts, ideas within ideas, and are not real in-and-of themselves, not as separate stand-alone entities. Once we accept that these ideas are not real in-and-of themselves, we will begin to see that they are nothing more than reflections of the same original idea of separation, just like all of the other symbols that make up this universe, including this universe itself.

The world that we experience is nothing more than the outward projection of our inward nature. To the individual, these projections are localized experiences and are the neutral reflections of what we project onto everything that we believe we perceive around us. Thus, the contents of what appears to be our personal life are only our own impressions of these object symbols – the things through which we attempt to identify ourselves. The projections are reflected back to us revealing what we reject inwardly. On a more global scale the collective consciousness is doing the very same thing we appear to be doing on a personal level. One nation's ideology filters and slants the perception of what seems to be another nation. In this manner, our personal conflicts that rise from our local projections are the same in like and kind as their global counterparts, just seeming smaller in scale. We are in a constant process of revealing to ourselves those places against which we have erected barriers to block out and deny "ownership" in favor of "independent selfhood".

From here we begin to see that which they reflect to us is what we have agreed to believe is damaged in us or resisted (judged) by us. We can then begin to accept them for what they are, rather than reject them for what they seem, and make them real in the mind. We can recognize that the actions never actually occurred in reality, not the way we think they have. We do this to invoke the healing processes that we, or the seeming fragments we represent, have agreed to believe that we need. The fragmenting process that *is* the ego identity has produced an illusion of equal parts horror to beauty. Like a Yin and Yang of light and dark presence. This way, when we seem to become disenchanted and appear to be rejecting the illusion, we see something that implies the essence of hope. These glimmers of hope are usually just enough to keep us coming back for more, while the horrors never seem quite enough to sever the tie that we use to bind us to the illusion of this false universe. Our false nature only accepts real change once we have exhausted every avenue of imagined change we fabricate for ourselves out of our images of the past.

Eventually we can bring ourselves around to recognizing this unified paradigm of experience, where *everything* we are experiencing is essentially *one-and-the-same* lesson. One lesson on how to release the identification of self that arises to counter these questioned events. We will begin to see there are no horrible acts, no disease, no suffering, just cries for Love, disguised as these objectionable effects, calling from one estranged fragment of ourselves to another. We are calling out *to* ourselves, to *find* ourselves, *within* ourselves. We will see that the only appropriate response to such actions or events is Love, not judgment. That would mean to fully and completely accept all that we perceive, as equal and one with what we consider as self. Then we can begin to see only innocence, purity and wholeness in all that we appear to encounter as our accepted reality. There is no tragedy and there is no triumph. There is only a menagerie of symbols that appear to us as events to which value is applied under the guise of the ego identity. Values that this assumed identity has agreed to abide by, and through which, it pretends to know itself.

These lessons, so-to-speak, will become more and more self-evident if we fail to recognize them at first. They will continue to repeat themselves in what will appear to us as various forms, until we *do* recognize them. Each seeming iteration of the lesson will appear to us in a more and more intense or amplified manner until it would seem impossible for us to dodge it or ignore it (yet sometimes we still try to). For some, this point isn't reached until their seeming life is in total ruin. At that point, they simply throw up their hands and proclaim something to the effect of, "I give up" or "I can't fight this anymore". Others find ways to compromise or turn off that part in them that cares through alcohol, drugs, and too many other forms of distraction to number. They believe that they have found ways to sidestep the lesson in many of its forms. In doing this, they are forced to meet it in some imagined middle place, but they can never be truly happy with their compromise. They have simply agreed to push on through levels of conflict that they feel justified in opposing and deny the rest.

Soon, however, we will be completely aligned with the presence of our Authentic Identity as it works through us (the seeming fragments) to the awareness of what we truly are. We will come to see that every seeming circumstance, situation and event in our perceived lives are a part of a very basic and fundamental *lesson* (revelation) who's every outcome is always an indication of our oneness. Only in the recognition of our oneness will we find the true nature of peace, and only through the kind of forgiveness that absolves the act from ever having happened will we ever recognize our oneness and find peace.

The point of our seeming journey is to realize that there is no journey and to forgive the idea that there ever was.

• Chapter Nine •

What Path Are You On?

•

How many times have you heard people make reference to the "path they (or you) are on?" Quite a number of times I'm sure. There are some interesting things that I have come to recognize about these "paths" that I would like to share with you. First of all, ALL paths are of the ego identity as each and every one of them is a conditioned or disciplined state of the mind in attempts to find something. The mind can be made into anything we can imagine. The mind can be made to conform to any imagined cultural, religious or political persuasion. Any number of things can be done with the mind. You just need an adaptable system of education and a cunning strategy for manipulation. The oldest and most cunning strategy being used is the idea of reward and punishment. Society rewards cooperation or conformity and punishes non-cooperation or non-conformity. That is, with the exception of those places where the non-conformity is deemed sympathetic to the established system and appears to be a potentially new path for future forms of conformity and control to exploit.

The fundamental premise here is "forever seek and never find". It would seem that the core flaw to this "path" logic is the seeking itself for there is nothing to find. Yet everyone (well, almost everyone) keeps telling us to seek. What is it that we think we are seeking on these paths, enlightenment, wholeness, God? There is nothing in any aspect of our realm of possible experience here in the world of form that is not imagined into focused manifestation by us. That's right. Anything that you are capable of experiencing while incarnate is purely of your doing (not the "you" that is reading this book, the "you" that is *of* the Authentic Identity – The Dreamer). The Dreamer is presenting through the ego identity in what appears to us as infinite modes of expression, one of which is the "you" that is being experienced as "self" (from your point of operation). What is it that you (the "you" reading this book) hope to achieve or become by following some "path"? What is the assumed ultimate outcome or goal?

We seek because other humans who were also trained to seek trained us this way. Seeking implies that there really is something out there that needs to be sought and found. It implies that there is something that we actually lack and that if we don't find it we are incomplete – inadequate. It is the ego identity that is incomplete and inadequate, and being just an idea, it lacks any content and thus will never appear complete. It is the ego that is served when we seek and keep on seeking because as long as we are seeking, our focus exists solely in the seeming outer world of form that confirms and validates this false sense of self. This keeps us wrapped up in the illusion and hypnotized by its seemingly limitless complexity. As we seek, every tidbit that we find only suggests another tidbit just a little further down that same path (or some related path). So we push on and on under the mistaken idea that we are genuinely accomplishing something of value, when in actuality our personal identification with the illusion of accomplishment is keeping us right where we are. We never make any real progress – just the illusion of progress in this sense.

We cultivate our paths and marvel at our cleverness in identifying with them and learn to recognize similar paths in others. When we find paths that compliment our own, we call them "friend". When we encounter paths that conflict with ours, we call them "enemy" or "rival". This is no more accurate than spilling a glass of water onto the ground and suggesting that the drops that splash toward the north are friends with each other and the drops that splash toward the south are friends with each other, and these two groups "north" and "south", being decidedly opposed, are enemies or rivals one to the other. This is the same logic we use when judging human compatibility according to the seeming path it would appear one or another is choosing to be on. Yet this is exactly what the ego identity does. It separates everything. It separates everything into two main camps, preferred and not preferred and then attempts to surround it's self with only that which is seen as preferred.

Once again, here, the majority of the teachings step in and claim things such as, "All paths lead home" and "All paths are equal", or my favorite, "Your *true* spiritual path". The only one of these that contains the potential of any wisdom at all is, "All paths are equal", but not for the reason one might think that such a thing is claimed. All paths are equal because all paths eventually come to a dead end. All paths are the product of the ego identity and therefore are not real and lead us nowhere while perpetuating our attachment to seeking. The ego identity has a hay-day classifying, labeling and judging every little twist and turn that it pretends to discover and imagine as its "guidance" – guidance from where to where? You are trying to get home, however you are only "dreaming" that you are not home. In reality you have never left home, only in the dream do you believe that you have strayed, and the dream is purely an illusion. It is a dream and nothing more.

The whole idea of a path is that you are actually some quantifiable reality located somewhere within some equally quantifiable containing environment and that there is actually somewhere else that you need to be other than where you are. The branches of a tree are like paths – the trunk being the foundation and being-ness. The branches all flow (draw our attention) away from the center of our being, and each one ends without ever resolving the separation. Each branch (path) behaves like a tree (localized solution) unto itself. They are like distractions between the roots and the tip of the tree. During our seeming lives, we may change our path many times from one illusory dead end branch to another illusory dead end branch. The most common reason for changing paths is that the dead end is reached and the path is exposed as a shortcut to nowhere. Only the trunk reaches the zenith because it alone never left the center – the direct connection to its roots.

There is no path "home" because we have never left home. In fact, there is no such thing as "away from home". There is no path to anywhere because when you are already everywhere and therefore encompass all, there is nowhere for you to move *from* or *to*. Only the ego embodies the essence of separateness, individuality and smallness which expresses as an extension into space and time. The ego identity is a part of the illusion in which it moves and breathes and takes its very existence. It is but an idea, a construct within the framework of an instantaneous thought within a thought within a thought. Like a dog chasing its own tail, the ego keeps us involved in these seemingly endless pursuits of something else, something more. There is nothing else – there is nothing more. As long as we believe that there is a place we need to be, a goal to achieve, or a Spiritual level we must attain, we have already blinded ourselves. We will remain captivated by these useless pursuits in this false universe serving the false god (ego) until we invoke our true vision.

We spend so much of our time contemplating this supposed path we seem to be on that there is little room for anything else. We wonder if it is getting us to where we have imagined it is that we need to be. We spend countless hours manicuring our paths and trying to smooth the way for our effortless passage into some imagined enlightenment or at least something we perceive as better, or more valuable, than where we are now, or why would we pursue it. We go about creating every kind of belief structure to support and validate our paths and prove how our personal path is right and the other guy's path is wrong (or at least not as right as our own path). These seeming paths are nothing more than another way of separating ourselves from others, and an attempt to demonstrate how special and clever we are. All of these things are nothing more than further expressions of what we grant to this idea of an ego identity. They are but further examples of the one idea of separation experienced as many.

When we see someone who appears to be ailing, we quickly offer up our diagnosis as to exactly what it is that we perceive as being wrong with them. We will often offer up some sort of remedy in the form of a path correction to relieve their condition. If you just did this, you wouldn't suffer; if you just had that, you would finally be free. This usually means suggesting that they consider doing as we do because we believe that it's working so well for us. However, a path correction will never really address the cause of suffering, only the symptoms, and only momentarily. The ego identity wants as many allies as it can recruit in order to validate its own seeming path. So given any opportunity, the ego will suggest that those seen as ailing should "come join me". The ego suggests that it has the answer. However, all it has is the idea of an answer which leads to nothing more than more questions. It will never lead to a resolution. It simply cannot because there is no resolution. What we can do is accept that there is no way to improve what is already perfect and release the belief that we can (and the imagined need to).

Religions and Spiritual followings of pretty much every persuasion have been employing the path paradigm for centuries. We have imagined the ego identity with an insatiable need to be right, and the ego wants what is perceived as other ego identities to agree that it is right. We want it to be "right"; after all we are trusting this dark nature to hide us from our true selves. So the ego proclaims its rightness to the world, and those whom echo it back are drawn into the "flock". Through these measures we create every known organized religion and social organization. The ego identity will surround itself with every form of self-validating idea it can imagine and then identifies with each and every one of them as proof of its existence. All of this only serves to codify the idea of separation and the seeming reality of what appears to be our individual, or even our group, paths. That is not to say that all scriptural writings are false or duplicitous. However, I don't feel that they were originally produced by their authors for the expressed purpose of founding a dogmatic religious discipline.

Our path can seem fun and rewarding or our path can seem tragic and sorrowful. It's all up to the thought system that we apply to it, and as well, how deeply we are invested into it and its outcome. We can sit and marvel for hours or even years about how clever and crafty our path is, or has been. None of this will manage to get us any closer to our truest destination, because no path leads to our ultimate goal. That is because our ultimate destination isn't a destination at all. There is no journey involved in getting there. It is a sense of recognition, not an act of achievement. That is the one and only requirement that will awaken us to the awareness of that which always just "is", and that is to recognize it.

So why do we imagine so many different paths, and why do we place so much importance on each of them? The ego nature is fear and the idea of being stranded or lost expresses what this fear means to us. No matter how it arrives on our doorstep, to acknowledge this fear is to admit that the ego identity is a blind guide leading the blind follower. Therefore, any path that we perceive creates the illusion of great value by suggesting some sort of progress in the form of the acquisition of the path's various relative milestones. We chart our course and navigate it as best we can, and we stick with it come hell or high water. However we will just as quickly drop one path for another when the path we are on dashes us against the stones one too many times or we see something more attractive to us on another path. No matter how many times we change paths to "fulfill our purpose" in life, we swear that the path of the moment is *the* path. Through our egoic certainty we blind ourselves to any genuine alternatives.

The path *of* the moment keeps us from being *in* the moment by keeping us focused on where our current path promises to take us, rather than where we actually are. This is just another way we empower the ego identity to distinguish us from some, while allying us with others. We create yet another symbol of yet another layer of separation between what is seen as self and what is seen as not self. We also justify our lack of forgiveness and our right to attack others because "they are doing it wrong". They must be, because they're doing it differently than we are, and we most certainly must be doing it right! The ego identity will utilize any number of excuses or justifications to keep us focused on our particular paths rather than on our true presence.

Why then do we imagine so many paths? What problem is it that we believe we are solving? It would seem that rather than solving a problem, we are sustaining (or creating) a problem. If the ego identity can appear to have a purpose that can be extended into both the past and the future, we will be distracted from experiencing the present moment. By being so immersed in our delusions, we fail to recognize that we are simply perpetuating the ego identity without any consideration as to its actual usefulness. As the old saying goes, when you're up to your butt in alligators, it is rather difficult to remember that your objective is to drain the swamp. If the ego identity can keep us distracted and occupied with anything other than what *really* matters, we won't stop to question the motives *driving* the insane mission.

If in fact there were such a thing as a "path to salvation", it leads only from where you are to where you are, as no movement at all is necessary or even possible. Any indications to the contrary are purely of the ego identity and wholly of the illusion. All of our ideas about self-improvement are manufactured by the ego identity, as it and it alone is capable of embodying the illusion of change. Change and evolution are purely of the ego identity and not present within the Authentic Identity. Any attempt at self-improvement, as well, leads only from what you are to what you are, as no *real* transformation is necessary or even possible. It is not possible because that which already is everything cannot be "transformed". The ego identity will send us on numberless journeys seeking every kind of "personal change" imaginable. The ego subscribes to the belief in sin and perdition and sees all as sinful and needing redemption from something that is beyond, something that is outside of the localized "self".

As long as we seem to experience a world of separation, we are following the ego's lead. As long as we follow the ego's lead, we are blind followers being led by blind guides on a never-ending search for that which cannot be found. Part of the problem it would seem we are encountering is that we are using the body and our physical senses as our tools of investigation and determination. Also, it would seem that every time we reach a dead end on our path, rather than question our method of seeking, we simply turn and begin seeking in another direction. Without any real hesitation, we just charge down some seeming new path. The same mechanism in us that keeps us blind to the uselessness of *any* path we choose is the same mechanism that keeps us forever trudging along on these paths.

It is only once we see the futility of any and all of the paths we have chosen, that we begin to see that what we are cannot be found by "seeking". It is found by being receptive to what already is, rather than being resistant to it. We could endeavor to facilitate within us a willingness to recognize what it is we believe that we are seeking and release it into the Spiritual connection that binds our human-ness to the Authentic Identity. In turn, our Authentic Identity will make the desired revelations to allow our Spiritual vision to see the truth (fact) of the matter. Without this release we will see only with the body's eyes. We will see only the illusion, and the illusion serves only to keep us entrenched within the prison of this dualistic thought system that the nature of a divided mind produces. Essentially, we are holding our seeming selves captive within the confines of an idea of which we are the source.

When I refer to someone's "path", what I am referring to is, in fact, the very life that they appear to be leading and the circumstances and events that appear to come to them in the assistance of their awakening. On the other hand, I am not referring to some imagined "spiritual journey" of transformation or discovery that they are undertaking. For me, a path is not something that we follow or pursue but more something that we simply stand witness to. This is because we are always in continuous communication with that which we truly are and to the degree that we become aware of this connection, we cease to invest in the idea of separation from it. Likewise, the less we are aware of this continuous connection, the more we believe that we are bodies amongst other bodies living very separate and secret lives, one from the other.

We can read the books, watch the movies, attend the seminars, and at the end of the day, we are no better off than when we started. In fact, we are generally less in touch with our own thoughts and feelings, having been pushed and prodded in every direction and being told what it is we lack and must *do* to correct these seeming shortcomings. What is more, we are also becoming increasingly confused about the thoughts and feelings of those we have chosen to call teachers. The only true teacher resides within us, and we need only look there for our every lesson. The only help that an outside source can provide to us is through its encouragement to look within and only within for our teaching. This is what I encourage you to do. Don't listen to me; listen to yourself, or more specifically, *your* inner teacher. This is something that only you can know and only you can acknowledge within yourself.

Am I suggesting that you should give up your path? No, that is not the point to this at all. Your "path" must be servicing some belief or need you perceive within yourself or you wouldn't feel the need to "follow" it in the first place. Therefore, until you recognize what this seeming need is, you will simply continue to repeat this behavior until it is released. It is by recognition that we become free of our self-imposed limiting factors and not through detachment, rejection, denial, suppression or resistance. These are nothing more than negative attachments at the behavioral level. This is because in these ways, the thing denied becomes that thing we attach to by claiming we will keep "that" at bay. In this manner, we are agreeing that the thing or condition is in fact real and must be manually suppressed or put to the background out of our way. This is like trying to become "free" of some old undesired clothing by simply putting them into a box in the attic. We aren't really free of them. We have simply moved them to a less observed location in our consciousness. In this way, we do not become free of them at all.

What I am suggesting is a more honest appraisal of just what it is that the path you believe that you are on serves within you – How is it helpful? – What does it achieve? For as long as you believe that it is leading you somewhere useful, you would benefit from determining where that seeming useful place is. If where it is leading you requires any sort of needed "change" or "transformation" in your "self" it becomes clear that it serves the ego thought system and nothing more. This is because there is no change possible to your Authentic Identity, which is complete and whole needing nothing. The Authentic Identity is, by its very nature, already all encompassing and does not transform, at least not in the traditional sense. Only the ego identity is capable of change and transformation, as it is always seeking ways to "adapt" to what it perceives as its environment and the imposed limitations and conditions therein.

All conceivable paths suggest accomplishment or transformation of some sort. Each and every one represents, or is a symbol of, some sort of attachment that we willfully maintain with some portion of the illusion. Something about it is attractive to us in that whatever it seems to serve is trying to tell us from where it is that we still derive a false sense of self.

Whatever it is that the path is serving within its follower indicates either some form of perceived lack or a call for healing. In either case, the seeming path will not get us "home". They may serve as a tool to expose some of the blocks that we have put in place to keep us from realizing that we are already home, but they cannot get us to where we already are. However, we tend not to perceive them in this manner. Instead our paths distract us by keeping us focused on pleasing (or regrettable) past events and anticipated (or feared) future events. All of these distractions simply keep us believing that there is something to be accomplished or achieved in this world of form that will finally set things right and free us to our rightful place in eternity. We'll finally have peace when ... you fill in the blank.

Not only is there nothing that you need to do, there is nothing that you can do. That is not to say that we should sit idle and remain completely dormant waiting to be released from this illusion. What I mean by this is that anything you do, or don't do, has no affect whatsoever on that which is "True" and "Real". The idea you can take away with you is that when you redirect your intentions toward the peace of God, there is no chance of failure, so relax and just be aware of the ride rather than resisting the moment and trying to steer. Along this same vein, as we persist in this place, our presence *to* the moment will drastically improve our experience *of* the moment. So really, we can merely be willing to receive such understanding and be willing to extend receivership to all seeming others as well.

We cannot *make* ourselves holy, nor can we *correct* the seeming error that appears to hold us bound. This is because the thought system that we are attempting to use to free us from our suffering is the same thought system that binds us to the suffering in the first place. Thus, we must decide that as humans we are unable to break free of humandom. However, we can allow that which we *really are* to reveal glimpses of Truth's reflection to us through the medium of the Spirit. For the outward expression of what we appear to be, here in the world of form, is *of* the world of form, and on its own cannot rise above that which it is. That which is our true Identity knows its own and can extend our understanding beyond our earthly confines.

You need not take even one step from where you appear to be right now to find peace. You need not read one single book, watch any movies or attend any seminars to become aware of your Authentic Identity. This awareness is the same state that many call "enlightenment" and suggests that you must attain it through some sort of ongoing discipline. That would represent an exclusive thought system which would exclude any whom do not seem to employ some discipline that will achieve this lofty goal. Additionally, the "book", "movie" and "seminar" may never avail themselves to some, and this would mean that they would be left behind for want of the price of admission or even the opportunity to attend. This simply cannot be so. We do not "attain" enlightenment, for that would be to suggest that it is somewhere else and that it must be "sought" and "found" to be had. We cannot become that which we already are, but we can become aware of its presence by releasing the blocks that we hold dear and worship in its place.

As I have stated already, you cannot become that which you already are, and that which you already are is already complete, whole and perfect and does not evolve or change. You are infinite and all encompassing, and there is nothing that you lack. You cannot be improved upon, nor can you be diminished in any way. To suggest that you can be changed in any way is to suggest that something outside of the Creator is more powerful than the Creator and can override Its authority and alter Its Creation. So you can relax knowing your path is complete and that you are "home" safely joined and in Perfect Oneness with your Source. Nothing can ever change this under any imagined or unimagined circumstances or events. There is nothing that you can do to make yourself (Authentic Self) anything but what you already are – perfect, whole and completely innocent, now and forever.

It is through an investigated life that we can find real peace and freedom from the torment and suffering offered to us through the opinions of the world. So let us dismiss the path and remember that we are the Truth. Not these human forms that we are

137

experiencing, but that which gives rise to all of these natures that that seem to experience form at all.

• Chapter Ten •

Be Love

•

"Be Love". To some, this comment is as foreign as saying, "be amplitude" or "be knowledge". Most people can reconcile the human concept of being *loving*, but "be *love*", what does that mean? Love is "give" not "take" and not in the shadow of some pity or self-aggrandizement. Certainly love does not come with any agenda of charity or the unspoken pretense of some future reciprocation. To be love means to put the apparent needs of others before what would appear to be our own needs. It means to be of continuous service to all. It means we do not give continuously of ourselves in expectation of some future return or in terms of any benefit toward what might be perceived as our local self. We give because it is what we are compelled to do from the deepest sense of our truest nature. If we examine this concept from the perspective of the ego identity employing the ego's thought system, this will seem quite insulting if not completely insane. The ego thought system wants to bargain, trade and barter to secure the most "self-advantageous deal" it agrees to recognize. The ego wants to be paid what it perceives as its rightful dues, in full – cash on the barrelhead.

Real Love does not discriminate as to whom it flows. Like the sun (as a metaphor), Love shines on all equally, not only those that please us outwardly. It's sort of like the story of the Yogi who was walking along a stream with a friend and sees a scorpion that had fallen into the water. The Yogi reaches down to rescue the scorpion, and the scorpion stings him. He reaches again, and again the scorpion strikes. The Yogi repeats his attempts for a few minutes, when his friend finally says out-loud, "you're trying to save the poor thing, why does it keep stinging you?" To which the Yogi replies, "because, that is what scorpions do." His friend then asked, "why, then do you keep trying to rescue it?" To which the Yogi relied "because, that is what I do." In other words, we cannot let the actions of another determine how we will act in return. In this same way, real Love does not pick and choose where it is applied based on ones determination of which are suitable to Love.

As humans, we have scarcely even a shadow of an idea, of what real Love is. The ego takes the lowest level of emotional suffering we recognize and calls it love and looks upon the highest level of emotional suffering and calls it hate, terror or fear. It is only by the comparison of one to another that either of these takes on any meaning. We never once pause to look upon what it *really* is we are accepting into belief. Rather than allowing ourselves to release the endless cycles of suffering and lack we experience as our reality, we simply redefine the perceptions we entertain about them. The ego manufactures all of its self-proclaimed knowledge about all of the things in our seeming world by their comparison to something else. Our human perception of love is no exception to this ego rule, as we claim to know love through fear by comparing one to the other. This, however, will never work.

We have, through this judgmental process, created numberless hierarchies of comparisons of things to justify what we claim to like and want, as well as what we do not like and do not want. All of the supposed knowledge of this world is nothing more than agreeing to one illusion or another. As long as our system of prejudices satisfies our imagined needs, we keep it intact. If at any time one of our perceived needs is threatened or not met, we simply get rid of the corresponding prejudice and replace it with another one that we believe will accomplish what the old one did not. In short, we compromise.

Real Love is beyond the scope of our learning while we accept the ego thought system as reality. For real Love has *no* sense of *any* sort of self and recognizes *no* hierarchies of *any* type, even in the most infinitesimal of scales. And most certainly, Love *never* compromises. All real Love is complete and whole, knowing no boundaries or limitations of any kind. It graciously gives everything and asks for nothing in return. Love is not a thing, nor is it the state of a thing. Love is not an emotion, affection or an intimacy. Love is a pure nature that liberates our perceptions of others and allows us to see our brothers and sisters as perfect having no blemish or flaw, without exception.

Love does not select its recipients, as it is freely extended to all. Like the story of the Yogi, love does not retract itself if seemingly met with hostility. Love knows that the only response to anything, real or imagined, is Love. For that which is real will always proceed out of Love, and the only proper response to this is Love. Anything proceeding from that which is not real is proceeding from the illusory ideas of separation and fear and is therefore always a *call* for Love. The only proper response to this, as well, is always Love.

The ego knows nothing about what is real. It knows only the illusion and the machineries of self-delusion that operate therein. The ego's dualistic thought system at the behavioral level knows only negotiation, bargaining and compromise. It seeks to secure the best "deal" it can engineer in an imagined world of limitations and restrictions. To the ego, all love is at a cost, and therefore, no love is simply free. Love is to be used as leverage while bargaining, or as a means to an end. To the ego thought system, love is how we treat someone when we want something from them.

To the ego, love is just another tactic on the avenue of negotiation for the imagined power over others. According to the ego's understanding of the world, love always has a victim, and no one is simply worthy of love without restriction. To duality, love cannot exist without fear. Unconditional love is absolutely non-existent in the false imaginings of the ego identity because everything is conditional in the world of form. As well, there is always something that must be held back, something that is kept off of the bargaining table, a sort of escape route for when things go wrong. And according to the ego's understanding of love, things will always go wrong.

To "be Love" is not nearly as difficult as it may seem or sound. It is the ego's perception of the commonly held idea of love that becomes difficult and complicated. Under the ego's influence, everything becomes clouded in mystery and over-shadowed with clandestine images of fear, sacrifice and constant defense of some imagined weakness. With real Love, there is no need for defense of any kind, because there is no weakness of any kind. As stated previously, Love knows no attack because Love only shares, it never takes. True Love is *real* and therefore cannot be genuinely threatened. Love has no needs of any kind and knows no lack or limitation. So if what you are experiencing as love has needs or restrictions, then it isn't love. Under this pretext it is reduced to some sort of negotiation or barter. Love is not an emotion, nor is it an emotional state. It is a way of looking at all of existence with total acceptance without reservation and without judgment.

If we can agree to release our need to extract *anything* we believe holds value in the world of form from *any* of our relationships with *any* of the people or things in the world of form, we simply become Love. We then share that which we are, equally and completely with all, and expect nothing in return. Every relationship that we experience is of equal worthiness and is deserving of our full appreciation. As soon as we place one above another, we have fallen back into the ego's thought system and the illusion of separation and its hierarchies. In defense of this error we assume an all too familiar defensive posture as to why one is better than another. That is because hierarchies involve judgment and judgment requires defense, where Love does not. Once we agree to perceive levels, we must defend why certain ones are above and others are below, even if only in our own apprehension of the relationships. Love and judgment can never coexist, as the presence of one absolutely denies the presence of the other. In a way similar to how light transforms darkness, Love transforms judgment and fear.

If we look upon our brothers and sisters with the ego's eye of separation which opens us to contempt, we will always find some reason to mistrust and some reason to defend. But what is it that we are defending, and what are we defending against? A defensive posture is always in response to some perceived sense of weakness or vulnerability; something that we perceive as being in need of protection from some perceived external threat. No one can perceive an enemy unless they are an enemy. So, it would appear that we are defending against the possibility of seeing ourselves (the Authentic Identity) in those we view as "others" or "enemy".

All conflict arises from within our seeming selves, not between the self and some seeming other. Therefore, within all conflict, there are no good guys and bad guys – only the idea of enemies and they both exist in the one mind. Any distinctions we entertain about either are solely based upon the side of the fence on which we happen to find ourselves taking preference. All of this conflict exists only within the ego's thought system and nowhere else. This is because the thought system of the ego knows only conflict and attack. It knows only peace through power and love through control.

When we begin to step outside of the idea of a separate and distinct self, we begin to realize just how much we share in common with those we perceive as others or enemies. There is no self and there is nothing that is other than self. There is only that which I have referred to as the Authentic Identity – The Identity that is no identity. We are, all of us, the "Buddha", "Christ" or "only begotten Son", the one offspring, the one Creation of the one Creator. I, for one, prefer not to assign gender to such a presence as gender itself implies duality. There can be no duality when we are talking about a Perfect Oneness. There is no gender in the absolute.

In such a reality, it becomes quite obvious as to why Love is unconditional and asks nothing while sharing everything. There is nothing that is withheld *by* our presence *from* our presence. Any Love that is, is shared, equally and completely, within the One Presence. Therefore, nothing can be "lost" or "taken". Only in illusions can such ideas seem to exist, and even there they must be given away, not taken. Illusions are not real and therefore these ideas as well are not real. Yet we allow these illusory ideas to directly influence our every decision.

Only within the illusory thought system of the ego identity resides the idea of a separate self that must "get" *anything* from *anywhere* or *anyone*. The ego has no idea what reality is. All it does is entertain its own thoughts about what is real as though the thoughts themselves are the thing. Reality is as foreign to our false sense of self as personal or separate possession is within a Perfect Unity. To deny one in order to reward another is the foundation of the ego thought system – forever seeking and never finding. To the ego, whatever it is that it seems to seek will always reside in the *next* acquisition. It can never reside in the present moment, as the present moment is the only thing that even resembles real in this false universe. Not *real* according to its content, but real according to the fact that it is all there is to this universe – only *now*. To the ego, "the now" is lost to the idea of a past and a future, as these are what define the nature of the ego. It is never what actually *is* in the moment. It is always what *was* and always strives to become what *will be* when some imagined need is met.

Because of its involvement in maintaining a completely imaginary or illusory idea of an individual self, the ego is only able to perceive what a relationship is according to its own limited evaluation of it. The ego will measure what a relationship will bring to us, or take from us, in some imagined future. Or the ego will measure what a relationship has brought to us, or taken from us, in some imagined past. Because of this, it sees every seeming brother or sister as possessing some sort of retained guilt or blame for past transgressions or future threats. This perceived guilt or blame resides completely within the ego's thought system and not in those we perceive as others. It is an illusion, an imagined state that exists by the imagining of the separate self as justification for any attack one seeming self harbors against any other seeming self. Everything that our five physical senses present to our awareness only exists to reinforce the illusion and stand in testimony of the validity of its own false nature. We judge others according to what it is that they provide *to* us and/or what it is that they withhold *from* us. Through this

147

deluded thinking, our brothers and sisters become a source of acquisition or loss to us. They assume the roles of "enemy", "rival", "friend" or "ally", and one way or another they always come back to fear. We see them as being able to withhold from us that which we perceive a need for. We view them, not as they are, but rather as we imagine them to be. We see them as fulfilling our perceived needs or threatening the identity we currently extract from our relationship with them.

The Authentic Identity does not perceive any separate entities, and therefore, has no concept of withholding anything from any perceived aspect or sense of a separate self. Herein lays the "magic" of the new thought movement. What we, as humans, seem to experience as consciousness is but the ego thought system's perception of itself. Within this illusory thought system, what is held in the consciousness becomes what is experienced in what appears to be an exterior world of form. What we are (the Authentic Identity) has no agenda, no needs, and therefore no reason to get involved in determining what thoughts we (as seeming individuals) seem to have attached to and manifest into our human experience. This non-interfering nature is what we have mistaken for "free will" to choose. There can be no free will to choose where there are no *real* separate states to choose between. All choices in this imagined universe only exist in the imagination. We are simply choosing one illusory state over another, one illusion over another. And anything that we "manifest" into our experience of reality in this manner will be full of the same dark emptiness that we are trying to escape by manifesting it in the first place.

Mainstream teaching in the metaphysical community tries to manipulate our understanding of this non-judgmental, agenda-free nature of the Authentic Identity. They suggest the pretend notion that this is "God" or "Source", and this "Creator" is like some genie in the sky just waiting to grant our every self-indulgent and self-serving wish. They tell us if we just wish "correctly" there is nothing that can stand between our wishing and our receiving. Then they take what they see as having value in this world (money, and lots of it) to host seminars to "teach" you how to do your wishing correctly. What seems to be slipping through the cracks is the one simple question: "What do you *really* want?" Do you want to be set free from all worry, all suffering, any and all doubts about anything? Do you wish to awaken from this nightmare and return to the awareness of the Perfect Oneness from which you have never truly emerged or strayed? Or, do you want to remain a self condemned prisoner within this hell of a nightmare of suffering, anguish, birth and death, with a nicer pair of shoes, a better car, or a bigger house?

The whole "dream life" offered by the mainstream metaphysicians sounds real nice on the surface, but the underlying implications and what must be sacrificed to maintain that thought system is what we should be investigating. First of all, there arises the need to accept that God (the "IS") is separate from us and is our servant (or tyrant). It places the source of all of our suffering, known and unknown, into the self-same being that we also proclaim as our redeemer. This has effectively made these opposing ideas into one-and-the-same. The ego has done this by transposing Creator and Creation. Through the ego thought system we have placed the ego's ultimate idea of a self on the thrown of power in the Creators place, but only as an idea and not in reality as this is absolutely impossible. Even though they are always bonded as one, each of these, cause and effect, can never become the other.

That which made what we cherish as Life made also what we fear as death. This universe is the downstream effects of OUR *ideas* about thinking, not OUR Creator's thinking. This universe is a part of us, albeit a very small part of a non-helpful thought system, but a part of *US* nonetheless. Neither "good" nor "bad", it is but an idea within an idea. It is our doing, and thus it is completely reasonable that it be responsive to *our* impressions and apprehensions of it. Does it not stand to reason that any body of illusion that springs from our human mind would as well be responsive to the mind from which it takes its origin? To think that it would not, again, would be delusional.

Do you think for even a moment that the Creator created Its ONE Creation lacking the perfection that is the perfectly integrated compliment to its own Perfection? Is it reasonable to think that the Creator endowed a "special" few egos with the answers to all of the questions that seem to plague the whole of mankind and set them to the task of educating the rest of us, completing us, providing us with the missing portions that make us whole? The answer is NO as this is absolutely ridiculous. We lack nothing and we need nothing. Our true teacher resides within us as our eternal Spiritual connection to the Authentic Identity in the Perfect Oneness. It is the link that connects the Dreamer to the dream. It is the "Spirit", sometimes referred to as the Holy Spirit, Atman, The Voice of God, and many others. It is the presence within us that has never subscribed to our present state of duality. It is our tether to Truth, as all else is illusion and represents Truth not. But the one thing that is for certain is that it too is also one with us.

Love shares everything and asks nothing, thus even the most insane requests that stem from our imagined state of separateness will not go unanswered though we may not like or agree with the answer. Love knows that we the seeming many are actually ONE, within which an infinitely small idea of a thought is simply behaving like a dream within a dream. It knows that it is only a matter of awakening our deeper awareness of the nature of this dream that serves to free us. Therefore Love has no concept or need of intervention. Intervening would only accept that the dream was real and that some sort of intermediary third-party correction was necessary, that something was actually at risk. It would be to accept that there is something to do the intervening and at least two other things to be intervened between. In pure non-duality, no such separate "components" can ever be real. They can only be imagined and only in a mind that is asleep to itself. It is but one idea of a thought within a thought within a thought that is imagining this dream, which is but a dream within a dream within a dream itself. All of this exists in a dimensionless point of infinite potential. The infinitesimal aspect of us that is experiencing this dream within a dream is limitless and dimensionless existing in its entirety at every seeming point in this seeming third dimensional time-space reality.

We enter into a relationship with our natural loving state when we release the need to extract anything more from any moment, than it offers to us by its very existence. When I say a loving state, I do not mean that we start loving everyone and everything more, or each seeming person, or thing, more directly. I mean we simply love without condition or direction. We don't simply love people more, or love nature more; *we simply love more completely and without regard for any particular outcome or personal gain, benefit or cost.*

The simple fact that what is, *is*, becomes enough. Not because of *what* it is, but just *because* it is.

Without judgment applied to everything that we experience (good, bad, like, dislike), we find our true nature is all that we need. That is to say that all that we need is to enter into a relationship with what we already are and nothing more, or more to the point, nothing *less*. Anything else is illusion and serves only to keep us entangled in some mistaken identity we perceive as our own.

The only way we can even conceive of being anything that we are not is to assume the posture of imagining that we are something *less* than what we actually are. What we are is infinite and all encompassing. Therefore, it would be impossible for any intelligence to imagine *more* than infinity. This being self-evident in that no matter what is imagined in infinity, by definition, is already included. So, suffice it to say, the only way to imagine being in any way different than what we really are is to imagine being less. The ego has no real concept of infinity or the infinite. It can only apply its delusional thought system to what it pretends these things mean. It does this by imagining what they mean in relationship to its imagined "self". All that the ego can imagine is the separate and conditioned – that which is perceived as an objective reality constructed entirely of things from the past.

Eventually, the ego identity suspends nearly every human thought within this framework of self-imposed limitation. This is because by its very nature thought is a closed system that feeds entirely upon itself and thus can never escape itself. By logical progression, it places the same limitations on everything it perceives. Anything that involves the infinite or limitlessness confounds the ego, for no comparison can be drawn between that which it identifies as self with all of its limitations, and that which it *pretends* to imagine as the infinite, knowing no limitations. These two are so incompatible that the ego identity can find no common ground from which to draw a comparison. Therefore, it summarily dismisses the infinite from its delusional thought system altogether and substitutes its own limited concept of the infinite in its place.

It is not possible to be more than what we are, as well as it is not possible to be less than what we are. Even though we can never be more than what we are, we can become more than what we *thought* we were. As I stated earlier, it is not possible to imagine anything that is more than what we truly are, but we can in fact, imagine less. This can only be accomplished by splitting or dividing the appearance of what we are into seeming components or parts, and this can only be conceived of in the imagination. This is because, in reality, it is impossible to divide or multiply the infinite. Therefore, it is purely illusory to consider ourselves as anything other than what we truly are. We can deny it, but we cannot change it. The ocean can call itself a puddle, but this has absolutely no effect on the nature of the water that makes up its true being. The Authentic Identity is an all-inclusive being-ness knowing no exclusion of any sort, as any exclusion would surely preclude any infinitude. The ego identity, on the other hand, exists entirely within an illusory realm of exclusivity and limitation, without any real unity, knowing only separation, compromise and fear. Consequently, it perpetually finds the need to defend its perceived borders.

Love is what we become when we release everything that proceeds from memory that we think we know, and accept that as an ego, we truly do not *know* anything. This is because "knowing" is infinite and eternal as it subsides entirely in the instant. What the ego does is to "think" and "perceive", thoughts and perception are limited conditions stemming from comparisons made between seeming past events. We may possess what we have learned to call "facts" and "relational information" about this seeming universe, but information about an illusion is not knowledge. This so-called information is illusory as well, as it too is simply relational comparisons of things past. If we can but accept that, as humans, we do not know what anything in this world of form is for, as well, what the world of form itself is for, we can release our seeming selves from the iron grip of our own personal judgments.

When we look upon our brothers and sisters without judgment (without consideration of a past or a future) we can only see them as innocent and without fault. The only way one can be found to be inadequate or failing to "measure up", is by comparison to something believed to be other than self. It is when we attempt to extract something that we perceive as having value in the world of form from our current perception *of* the world of form that we are suggesting that we know what this world is for. We see it as a place that exists for the purpose of satisfying the needs of that for which we agree to seek. We see it as a means to fulfill that which we perceive we are lacking. This, too, is delusional.

We choose to believe that we can hide that which we truly are from others because we do not understand what it is that we truly are. As well, we fail to recognize that what we *truly* are cannot be *hidden* in the first place. We can deny what it is we are, and we can redirect our imagining to all forms of fantasy, but no matter how determined we are to avoid the experience of what we are it does not change it nor hide it. We then tend to project this lack of understanding out onto the world of form and apply it as blame to our brothers and sisters for all of the things that the world denies us. Seeing in them this lack of understanding of us that, in turn, justifies our belief in the necessity to hide that which we believe we are from them.

But in truth, it is our own lack of understanding of what we are that causes us to hide ourselves from ourselves, not from some "them". As long as we feel it is necessary to hide, we confine ourselves to a thought system that perceives lack and vulnerability, and our world shrinks as a result. The perception of both lack and vulnerability justify our belief that we need to protect ourselves *by* hiding. Can you see how this is a self fulfilling prophesy? Thought is a wholly closed system. It is a self-consuming system that is bent on keeping its imaginary self captive as prisoner within the self-same thought system that we believe is there to protect us.

When we stop hiding (which is useless in the first place) we find that we have no vulnerabilities needing defense in the first place. We are not hiding from the "others"; we are hiding from our fears about them and our current understanding of ourselves. There are no vulnerabilities to defend because in reality, there can be nothing held back in an all-inclusive state. Only in the illusion of separation does there exist the idea that there is something secret to find and capture or something to be kept secret and to defend.

It is like a dog chasing its own tail. Every time that he is able to catch it and clamp his jaws closed to secure it, the bite causes the dog to yelp in pain causing him to lose his grip and release his tail so he can begin to chase it all over again. It never occurs to the dog that he already possesses that which he appears to be chasing. If he would simply quit chasing his tail and inflicting injury to himself doing so, he would cease to have all of the frustration, pain and suffering that appears to accompany his imagined quest.

Release the need to possess, release the need to control, release the need to pretend that you know anything about how anything got to be where and what it seems to be. It is all an illusion fabricated in our imaginations imagination. Simply accept that it appears to be, and that there is no value in controlling it because it is temporary. Always remember that all that is temporary, God (the IS) did not create. All that is eternal is Truth, not illusion, and extends as a state of grace in Source. Love is eternal. If you simply allow yourself to be that which you already are without trying to form yourself into something that you are not, restrictions, labels and definitions fall away and in this moment you cannot help but be Love.

• Chapter Eleven •

What Makes Me Think this is an Illusion?

•

First of all, I will need to define what I mean by "illusion", or more importantly, what I mean by "real". Secondly, I will need to address limitation and its opposite, infinitude or completeness. These two ideas are the primary underlying factors that I see as being instrumental to any attempts at exposing this illusion for what it is. When we are talking about the "absolute", we are most certainly not discussing the realm of the "conditioned" and visa-versa. The absolute does not express in any form or it would cease to be the absolute, as it would be limited by whatever form or forms it assumed. The conditioned cannot be expressed in any manner other than by some identity it extracts through comparison to something else. Which means it subsides entirely within the idea of form bound by its conditioning and can never obtain to the absolute. Because of the

159

nature of this dialog, I will be taking certain liberties with the wording that may suggest contradictions to these core ideas. I hope that the reader will bear with me and exercise some insight and discernment while interpreting some of the passages.

When I speak of illusion, what I mean is that which is in flux or in transition – that which is temporal or the *product of perception*, meaning that it occurs in the mind and nowhere else. Therefore, I am referring to what is impermanent and only experienced, rather than what is eternal and gives rise to what is experienced. I could probably dedicate an entire book to the splitting of this single hair alone. As such, this chapter will be the condensed version of such a book. In light of this, I will refrain from being drawn into a full-blown discourse on the "reality versus non-reality of experience" debate. I will, however, briefly cover this aspect and its relationship to the nature of the illusion. This will more than likely prove to be the most difficult chapter that I will have written for this book.

What does it mean then, to be "in flux" or "in transition"? For my purposes here, it means that which is represented as a continuous state of change or metamorphosis. Therefore, the content of our perception is always transforming from one thing or state to another and never being complete or whole at any given state at any given moment. I realize that one could argue that what is experienced at any given moment is whole and complete and simply passing

160

from one state of wholeness and completeness to another. On the surface, this argument seems perfectly reasonable. However, it has at least one, perhaps not-so-obvious, flaw.

The flaw of which I speak is contingent upon one thing, and that is what you hold as your concept of the Creator. If the Creator (according to your concept) were infinite and limitless, then anything that appears to be a material creation would, by extension, have to be illusory or imaginary. Why do I say this? If something were to be considered infinite and limitless, then any seeming material or non-material reality would have to take its existence within this infinitude. Therefore, by extension, this infinite something could not be contained or maintained by a "body", as any physical representation or symbol of "self" or even "parts", would naturally be a limitation, and thus a contradiction to its own being. Thus, it would stand to reason that this infinite presence would have to be entirely non-material. If the infinite must be non-material, then any seeming material reality would naturally have to take its existence within it as an *idea* of material rather than any real and distinct material or substance. Therefore, any *seeming* material reality would actually have to be *non*-material, simply presenting the appearance of being material.

Staying with this line of reasoning for a moment, let us explore the nature of any seeming material presence. An infinite presence of limitlessness, being non-physical, would then have no extension into space or time as these would automatically impose an unnatural limitation. It would, then, have to exist entirely independent of such concepts. On the other hand, any seeming physical or material presence would be entirely an extension into space and time. It would depend completely on these ideas for it to be present any sort of form. First of all, it would have to *be* somewhere occupying the space required by the form. Also it would necessarily have to be there during *some* time frame having a beginning, duration and an end. For any concept of infinity to be considerable, it would have to represent as being dimensionless as the infinite cannot be measured. Having no extension into either space or time, this dimensionless essence would be more of a zero-point potentiality than that which we are accustomed to calling *infinite*.

When we think of the infinite, we usually conceive of any point in space and extend outward from that point in all directions, forever. This model requires that our concept of infinity must therefore express itself by an extension into space and therefore time. Space and time are, by their very nature, limitations on anything that would otherwise be considered as infinite. We don't necessarily see this because we are accustomed to thinking in terms of a third-dimensional, space-time reality as the *only* reality.

This is to suggest that some infinite presence opened up a space in which to express itself. This expression would be fundamentally limited by its *dependence* on space and time. Therefore, the infinite could only express itself in a limited state. This would be a direct contradiction to its own nature. In order for the infinite to "express its existence" this way, it would have to cease being the infinite. In other words, in order for any genuine material creation to exist, the Creator would have to cease to exist in its current form to make way for something other than the Creator.

If the Creator were to be considered as other than infinite and therefore "finite", it would also become definable and describable. If the Creator were to be finite, then its existence as well becomes finite. In other words, it would suggest that the Creator has a beginning and therefore by extension of reason, an ending. If the Creator has a beginning, then something, some presence, would have had to give rise to *it*. Something would have had to create it. Therefore, by this reasoning, we are not talking about "the" Creator, but some kind of artifact of creation itself.

This would only mean that we have not gone back far enough as to have considered the original Creator or "Absolute First Cause" which would necessarily be a causeless state of IS-ness. We would have simply stopped at some point within the seeming stream of perception and declared it as the "Creator". At some point, there has to be a presence, a being-ness, that cannot be defined, that cannot be described, that has no antecedent conditions, that simply IS. At this point we find the one and only Truth, the one and only reality. We find what gives rise to that which can imagine the illusion, which for us, passes for the truth, and passes for reality.

Lao Tzu states at the very beginning of his "Tao Te Ching": *from a translation*

> "*The Tao that can be trodden is not the enduring and unchanging Tao. The name that can be named is not the enduring and unchanging name.*"

That is to say, if you can walk the path, it is not the true path, and if you can call upon the name of God, it is not God upon whom you are calling. In as much as I find agreement with any texts, I find agreement with this. As I have stated elsewhere: all of the pathways through which we seek are equal in that none of them lead anywhere, except to the conclusion that what we believe we are seeking is *not* on the path *or* in the destination. The path to enlightenment and the enlightenment themselves are simply ideas within this illusion we call reality. I cannot say it enough times, that we cannot become what we already are. It is only due to the illusory nature of this dream (nightmare) and the errant belief in separation, and thus, the fragmented perception of ourselves, that we see enlightenment as elsewhere and in need of being sought and attained. Nothing is elsewhere because there *is* no elsewhere *or* otherness for that matter.

Anything that is of the One Truth is, by extension, of the absolute and therefore eternal and real. Anything that is imagined as not of the One Truth is, by extension, what is seen as the conditioned world of form, and is therefore limited, fleeting and unreal. Only the real exists. All else must therefore be imagined. All seeming material or physical presence is an extension into what would appear to be a third-dimensional, space-time reality, and is thereby bound to the laws and restrictions (limitations) that govern that seeming reality. No matter how limitless it appears to be.

Being restricted or limited, these seeming material objects must all be finite and temporary. When I say that they are not real, what I am inferring is that they, in-and-of-themselves, are not real. Our experience of them may seem very real, as an experience, but they themselves are not. Experience is bound by perception, and perception is not reliable for determining what is real and what is not. For within its own seeming *experience* resides the only source of information it has for making any determination, and therefore it can know of nothing else. Thus, according to it, its own experience *is* its only benchmark of reality. Again, information is not knowledge; it is only the ideas held about seeming things brought about by an imagined comparison to some seeming other things. No matter what it is we believe to be real, it is still our human brain and mind that provide us with all the information we have about the world.   This we arbitrarily accept as being completely accurate, truthful and real. We accept our thoughts about any given thing as being the thing itself.

Let's take a trip into a dreamscape with which we are all familiar – the dreams we have while we are sleeping.   When you enter into your so-called "sleeping" dreams, *who* or *what* is it that actually *enters* into the dream? I'll give you a hint ... No I won't, I'll just tell you. It's not the *"you"* or the *"self"* that you seem to experience while you are in the state we refer to as awake. It is the same presence that is the observer of your so-called thoughts while in the waking state that enters into your dreams and is the presence and awareness there.   That same "observer" or "awareness" is the "you" that is the idea of a self that you believe you are experiencing. It is a reflection within your imagined self of what it is that you believe you are.

When you enter into your so-called "sleeping" dreams, what eyes are you looking through to see? Your human eyes are closed and dormant. Therefore, there is no need for the input of so-called data from our physical eyes in order to produce the images connected with the phenomenon of "sight". What is even more intriguing is the idea that these seeming images appear just as real to us as any images our "eyes" supply to us. Thus it would seem that the evidence provided by our "sight" is no more proof that the experience is real than the mere idea of the experience itself makes it "real". Yet you will hear people say things like, "Seeing is believing", and "What you see is what you get". So we can see (no pun intended) that what we see may, or may not, be the product of the functioning of our eyes.

When you enter into your so-called "sleeping" dreams, what ears are you listening through to hear? Again, your human ears may well be receiving information from the place in which you sleep or even from beyond its boundaries. However, is this information actually being integrated into some experience? Or is it being re-interpreted into the dream? Or is it being disregarded altogether? In the dream experience, the sounds within the dream, such as people talking to us, active machinery, or even the sounds of nature, are providing experiences that are only imagined. These sounds, like the sights, seem just as real as the ones we experience while we are in what we call our waking state. Once again, as with our sight, we are confronted with the illusory nature of what it is that we believe we are hearing.

When you enter into your so-called "sleeping" dreams, what body are you using to move about and experience the dreamscape? Certainly not your physical body, as it is lying or sitting somewhere fully occupied in a state we call sleeping. Yet we experience ourselves the same way in our so-called dreams as we do while in the state called "awake". We experience ourselves in what appears to be the same ways through the same senses. During our sleeping dreams, we may encounter our own reflection in a mirror or on the surface of a pond, so we do see some sort of body. However, it isn't always what we expect to see. We usually appear as the self with whom we are familiar, however, we may appear to ourselves as an animal or someone we know (or don't know). In any case, we experience what would appear to be some sort of a physical presence. What we are actually experiencing are impressions in our human mind. I trust you are coming to the realization that our experiences are, in fact, wholly inadequate as indication of what is absolute and real.

Just what is the dreamscape anyway? It is an idea, just like the one we experience while we believe that we are awake. As a testimonial to the power of the idea of a mind, consider this: In your dream state you create, in imagination, an entire containing environment all of the way up to, and including, a complete cosmos (if necessary). Every flower, tree, pebble and stone, every blade of grass, leaf, and animal of any sort, and, in some cases, even things that are not seemingly present in what we agree to believe is our waking universe. All of these things are created perfectly as you expect them, exactly where you expect them, even if they seem to surprise you in their appearance. And no matter how bizarre or unusual they may be, they appear perfectly normal to us in our dreams.

Your entire cosmos takes form in your presence at the precise moment that the idea of a self appears to experience it. Nothing that is imagined is omitted. The quantum model of the universe widely accepted by modern science suggests that all existence is, in fact, contingent upon some form of observation. It is accepted that, at some level, we are the observer, and everything we believe we are experiencing exists because we are observing it. I believe this is referred to as quantum superposition when everything exists in a state of infinite potentiality until observation is entered into the mix and everything collapses into that which is the observed. That which is observed is also entirely contingent upon the understanding of the observer.

There is a mountain of data and evidence accepted and agreed upon by the scientific community in general that suggests that our seeming waking world is not different, in any appreciable way, from the seeming dreaming world that appears in our sleep state. The waking world appears to be more consistent than the sleeping world, but this too is contingent upon whether or not what we call our memories are created by the same process as the realities that are experienced.

If the consciousness fabricates what we appear to experience moment to moment, then how do we know that it doesn't fabricate the memories about what we appear to be experiencing moment to moment as well? That is to say, is it a package deal?

Consciousness outlines not only our entire reality in what appears to be every instance, but as well, it provides all of the memories that accompany whatever the experience dictates in what appears to be the very instant itself. All of the memories that are appropriate to what appears to have led up to and brought about each and every moment as we experience it. If this were to remain constant to the one and only moment and we retain no awareness of any of the seeming other abstractions of the one moment – the moment of which we believe we are aware will always appear real and valid to us even though it bares no resemblance to any other moment we have experienced. Our experiences do not occur in a linear fashion (sequentially), they occur all at once – simultaneously. Our perceptions of them are entirely linear and require some sort of continuity to make sense to the ego filtered thought system. The ego identity remains wrapped up in the constructs that appear to lead up to the moment (the past), and the constructs that lead away from the moment (the future), but never the moment itself.

The experience of continuity exists because there is only this moment, this instant, and no other. Thus, *as* we seem to experience many varied forms of the instant, there *is* still no other. In other words, every possible eternity exists simultaneously in the one and only instant. Every possible geometry of thought is present in what we have agreed to believe is the one and only mind (which is not a real mind, but only the idea of a mind). However, this one and only mind also contains the thought, or idea of a thought, and this idea of a thought continues this dividing process until multiple points of operation or "identities" portrayed as humans or something of the sort seem to appear. These seeming separate identities appear to the respective individual as possessing an independent mind with independent thoughts. This too, is just an illusion, spawned by the same idea of separation fully contained and complete in the one and only instant.

The waters are getting a little bit murky right about now and at the risk of engendering the concept of a sequence of events into the model I've been suggesting, it seems quite impossible to describe what follows without borrowing from this imagined principle. Therefore, I wish to beg your indulgence at this point. When I refer to a "first" split, or any "subsequent" split within the idea of a mind, the seeming splits, first, last and any seeming intermediate splits, are all simultaneous, not sequenced. They are present before any of them are ever experienced. How they are experienced as a sequence of "events" or as an extension into space and time would be impossible to properly communicate in any symbolic language known to man without suggesting a linear stream of events. It simply cannot be "expressed" otherwise. Any deeper understanding of it can only come from "experiencing" it first-hand. Even in such cases when these

171

experiences come to us, they are often misunderstood from our imagined human point-of-view and thus shrouded in mysticism. This misunderstanding is what allows us to believe in the illusion as reality and every supernatural power imaginable at play within it.

After what could only be described as the first split of the imagined mind, the seeming two resulting minds each became aware of the other as a reflection or extension within its seeming self. Since all possible contingencies must necessarily exist, the entire imagined mind simultaneously conceived them all. These contingencies range from the entirety of the imagined mind knowing that no splitting or fragmenting was possible, that separation could never occur, to the belief that every possible splitting and fragmentation *had* in fact occurred, and that separation was the only reality. From the fragmented idea of a mind the inner reflection being experienced did in fact appear as an independent "self" separate and delineated against the *infinitely divided* backdrop of everything else believed to be "not self". The contingencies of this one tiny little idea within an idea also include every possible gradient division imaginable between these two imagined extremes. All of this fragmentation occurs simultaneous without any extension into the idea of space or time. In fact, space and time are an extension (idea) into this infinitesimal idea.

Let me not digress down that avenue though, as it too is most certainly a book unto itself. Instead, let us return to the dream analogies to which I was referring earlier. Ask yourself, "Are you absolutely certain that what you are experiencing right now is real?" Aren't you just as certain that your sleeping dreams are just as real until you awaken from them? Have you ever had a sleeping dream that was so real that even after you woke, you still swore that it was real? Perhaps you even required a moment or two to shake it from your head to regain your "waking" perspective. We readily accept that we are the maker of the dreams that we have while we sleep. Yet we deny the nature in us that is the maker of the dream we are having while we think we are awake. Could this be that we have mistaken the "waking dream" for what is real rather than another layer of what is imagined? Could it be like looking upon an imagined reflection, but within part of the mind believing that we are not seeing a mere reflection, but are in actually seeing a "self"?

I'm sure that you can see where all of this is going. Whether we believe that we are asleep or we believe that we are awake, what we believe we are experiencing is occurring entirely in the imagined human mind and nowhere else. Whether we believe the information that feeds our perception about the seeming environment is being gathered by the five physical senses or being supplied by the imagination, the results are the same – we appear to be experiencing something that has been accepted as an external "reality", and we rarely if ever question it.

So, hopefully, you can see that no matter what appears to be the experience, no matter what appears to be the means by which it arrives, it is still all the same. It all boils down to a matter of perception. It all boils down to some sort of subjective interpretation. Whatever it is that we seem to be experiencing, it is still only what the imagined mind tells us is being experienced and nothing more (and who is this mind telling?). The only meaning it holds for us is the meaning that we give to it ourselves, in that self-same mind, in that self-same instant.

What we call "life" and all of the experiences that go along with it, from space and time to every seeming action we perceive within it or "during" it, are only the idea of thoughts within thoughts within thoughts. Everything we are so certain is real, is nothing more than what could best be described as an idea with all of its possible interactive geometries and variations – everything needed to validate its reality to us. All of this is represented simultaneously, even though the experience of it appears to be sequential or linear, and spanning over extended periods of time.

It is like holding a DVD in your hand. The entire movie is present, beginning, middle and end, all simultaneously (including every potential directors cut). It isn't until you add the "artificial light" (space and time) that the movie appears to take on an animated presence of its own. This presence is complete with conflict, dialog, action and emotion, but none of it is real. It is all just bits, ones and zeros, and nothing more. It isn't until the digital translator observes the bits and translates them into some sort of meaningful symbols and projects these symbols onto some sort of medium suitable for displaying the imagery, that any sort of sense is derived from the DVD's contents. What I am saying is that it is all just bits until the digital-to-analog translator converts it into pictures that it projects onto the video screen as comprehensible images. It could just as easily convert them into random gibberish and display scrambled static. In other words, it only shows us what the digital translator tells it to show us, and nothing more (sound familiar).

If we are the dreamer and the dream, then any ill will or animosity that we harbor toward anything is ultimately harbored *by* ourselves, *toward* ourselves. What it represents is that there is some thing or some quality about our unrecognized sense of self that we are failing to understand from our limited human perspective of being separate. We outwardly project that which we do not understand in hopes of freeing the imagined *self* from it. By projecting these aspects, we can then place the blame for whatever they represent in thought, on that which we perceive as being *not* self – as being some other. This errant understanding creates the conflict we appear to experience, and it is from here that all calls for healing are being made (again, this is an ego interpretation – a human point of view).

That is not to say that it is okay to run amuck. Actually, it suggests quite the opposite. All of our conflict and suffering comes from the idea of separation. It comes from the idea that *they* are truly separate from *us* and it is *they* that are responsible for everything that is *wrong*. Therefore we feel we are fully and righteously justified in punishing *them* for *their* transgressions. What we are missing is that it is *us* that we are punishing in the guise of *them*. Being a Perfect Unity or Oneness, there can be no *others*.

According to this model, "they" would then be just as justified in punishing "us" for the conflict and suffering that we impose upon "them" according to our beliefs. Thus the viscous cycle stands unbroken, and this paradigm of punishment and counter-punishment can continue indefinitely. It will continue as long as we embrace the "us" and "them" paradigm of thought. It will continue as long as we are choosing to judge as real rather than forgive as imagined these menageries that fill our experience. In this way each party is holding the other party guilty in their judgment of them and forever condemning both parties to this battle of unconsciousness that never ends.

All of this, of course, begs me to give voice to the point of view – *real or imagined, it is still the world we live in, and we have to make due with what we have. We have no choice but to suffer the bad, and rejoice the good.* This point of view still suggests that this world (our lives included) and all it seems to stand for in our thoughts and ideas about it, is being done *to* us rather than *by* us, and that it has real meaning in-and-of-itself, independent *of* us. It is to accept that, real or imagined, we are here and there is no way out. Except perhaps by some third party intermediary or Divine intervention ultimately designed by an outside source.

Even if we subscribe to another world in the "hereafter", we are not actually "escaping" the grip of this dream within a dream within a dream. No matter how many dimensions or "next" worlds we imagine, we are only moving from one state of the dream to another state of the dream. Until we understand that we are, in fact, the dreamer and that infinity only exists within us as an idea (it is not us that exist within infinity as a prisoner), we will remain imprisoned by the idea. It is like escaping (or completing) one maze only to find the exit of the one maze is simply the entrance to another maze. As long as we perceive this universe to be real, there is no limit to the number of mazes we can put in place for our imagined selves to escape or complete.

Let's finish this up by looking at the phrase "be in the world, but not of the world". To be "in the world" is simply a testimony to the fact that you represent some aspect of the idea of separation that has agreed to believe that it is a presence unto itself. If this were not true, you wouldn't be experiencing "here" in the first place. To be "of the world" is a deeper commitment to the idea of separation. In doing this, you have assumed the appearance of being one point of operation amongst many and view the rest as truly not self. Being "of the world" creates the illusion of "*us and them*" and sets the imagination's stage for all manner of seeming conflict both internal and external. Being "of the world" means to believe that the world created you through some biologically imagined process called birth.

So being *in* the world but not *of* the world is to accept the unreality of what appears to be the sustaining thought geometry (of whatever sort) rising from an equally unreal sense of self. A recognition of the thought geometry, the effect of which, appears to have produced the illusion of separate individual points of operation while at the same time releasing any attachment to the ideas and thoughts that fuel the illusion of separation that give rise to these seeming individualities in the first place. We recognize the illusion for what it is and nothing more. We see our neighbor as ourself. We do not see our goals as separate from any seeming others'. We do not see our will as separate from any seeming others', nor do we perceive our will as separate from the Creator's will.

Be "in the illusion", but not "of the illusion". Be "in the dream", but not "of the dream". When we sleep and dream, the dream does not create us, we in fact create the dream. We create all of it in its entirety, beginning middle and end, including every potential director's cut. It is the same with our waking dream. We create it. It does not create us. That which creates us does not participate directly in our dreaming nor our dream. It is aware of the dreaming, but it is beyond any construct or concept that any dream could even begin to contain or symbolically represent.

Picture a perfect mother that gently cradles her only child lovingly in protective arms. The child has drifted off to sleep and has begun to dream. At first the dream may well be pleasant and seem almost paradise-like. However, it soon turns quite ugly and fearful as we lose the memory of where we truly are and begin to believe that we are where we are dreaming that we are. This mother feels the unease of our torment within this nightmare of ours as we are having it, but needs not interfere nor intervene, not being concerned with the dream's content at all. She only awaits our awakening where we will find that there has truly been no moment (so-to-speak) that we have not been safely at home in our loving mother's embrace. And once awake, the dream vanishes back into the nothingness of which it has always been. At once we are returned to peace as we remember where we truly are and have always been.

• Chapter Twelve •

How Do We Awaken Within this Dream?

•

Once again I will be taking great liberties with the language in attempts to communicate the core ideas of this chapter. As I have stated again and again, language is simply unsuited for expressing such concepts. Therefore, I will be expressing these ideas under the umbrella of separateness, space and time, and various other illusory or imagined frameworks that we readily accept into fact in our everyday lives. The reader is urged to bear with me in this endeavor and exercise some level of discernment in translating.

I know in matters such as these, much can be lost in translation, but I am unfortunately put into a position where there are few to no options. So in those places where I appear to contradict my position on Oneness, please understand that I am doing so to avoid writing hundreds of lines of text in order to make a point that otherwise would take only a few words to convey by assuming the commonly accepted definitions of certain things. Even in this, I will be applying more text than might otherwise be needed to certain sentences in order to uphold the primary theme of Oneness where I am able.

The first thing in the process of awakening that I would suggest is to take full responsibility for our reactions to what we call our thoughts. Recognize that the only meaning that they hold for us is the meaning that we *give* them. The meaning of "life" is the meaning that we give it and nothing more. In-and-of-itself, life is but an idea, another aspect of the illusion. We have assigned so much significance to it that is has become blown completely out of proportion. We have come to worship the idea of life and its preservation above all else.

Life, as we know it, has become the central hub of our existence, rather than the peripheral, yet integral, geometry of thought that it actually is. Life and death as we know them do not actually exist, not in the way we think they do. They are but ideas about things or, more accurately, about the "states" of things. These are necessary constructs only within the idea of separation to lend continuity to perception. In order to maintain this illusion of continuity in our currently perceived state of separation there is a need to explain where any experience comes from and where it goes to when it appears to be complete.

If we are willing to accept that all meaning is supplied by us, it is then a small step to accepting that all content is supplied by us as well. We supply both the subject and the object, or the active and passive components of consciousness, and therefore we are the supplier of any experience consciousness relates to us *and* the consciousness that experiences the relationship itself. No matter how we attempt to define it, all experience is evaluated according to its relationship to some perceived self. As long as we hold this *self* to be real and true, all that it appears to experience through its senses, by our perception, will be perceived as real and true as well. Left unto itself, it is a self-fulfilling and self-perpetuating cycle of imagining, projecting and believing. Until we step back from accepting our experiences into belief as truth, we will continue to experience variations of the one idea of separation in its infinite forms, for what may appear to us as countless lifetimes.

Consciousness produces the images of the perceived world of form by imagining the combination and manipulation of seeming polar opposites. We, as assumed individuals, assign value to these images according to the polarities that are found to be more or less pleasing to the particular "self" doing the assigning. From that frame of reference, we identify with the state of balance found to be more preferable or profitable. We then attach any emotional state (happy or unhappy, etc.) to the degree to which the "preferred" polarity is being expressed or experienced at any given moment.

Somewhere along the perceived timeline, we will remember that there are no polar opposites as actual separate and exclusive expressions of reality. We will recognize them as nothing more than the symbols of the unreality that they represent in the imagination. The unreality of separation and duality always expresses through the presence of both sides of what appear as polar opposites. These polar opposites always occur together, never separately. What we perceive as separation cannot, and will not, ever exist in any genuine reality. Separation from our creator or each other is simply not possible in any real sense.

Even in this seeming place where separation appears to be real and true, we are still ever connected to our Authentic Identity. Within each of the personalities (or points of operation), there is, for the lack of a better description, a Spiritual connection (or feedback loop) of being-ness that is ever "active" so-to-speak, gently nudging us to awaken from this dream (nightmare) of unreality. This is what has brought about the errant theological belief that we are "Spiritual Beings", which in-and-of-itself places a limitation on us. However, it is reasonable to suggest that in this place, the world of form, The Spiritual presence is the closest essence to our Authentic Identity we can experience and remain incarnate.

Theology has pigeonholed us into an ego-based idea of spirituality that cannot exist as they propose it.

This body of theological power sits in the seat of both judgment and authority to proclaim us as less than acceptable, as falling "short" of God's mark, doomed to eternal hell if left to ourselves. Imbued with this fear, we must accept their implacable authority and their brand of guidance to lead us out of the darkness into which their false teachings have helped hold us in the first place. According to these teachers we also must accept these teachings as the "Word of God" and the only path to salvation. This is another perfect example of the phrase – "the blind leading the blind". We are attempting to free ourselves from the disturbance that our thoughts cause, by thinking about them. We have come to believe that our fears will protect us from what it is that we believe we fear.

Theology has been unwilling to admit, or has failed to look deeply enough to find, that the Spirit is not what we *are*. It instead is that which connects the dream self (what is experienced), to the Dreamer (what is experiencing). That is to say that the Dreamer pre-exists the Spirit. The reason for this theological error or omission is that theology looks (or admits) only to the explanations that support the particular theology. Each theology remains at odds or opposed to any other theology or philosophy that disagrees with, or contradicts the tenets of its own discipline. This is especially true if the given philosophy risks exposing any fraudulent nature within the theology as nothing more than the distractions of the ego thought system that keep the seeming individuals forever searching for some elusive doorway that ultimately leads to nothing more than another illusion. Like I stated earlier it is like a maze whose exit only leads into another maze.

That which frees people from the need for theological teachers, like awakening to the internal teacher that gives rise to all of us, does not support theology – it dissolves it. External "God worship", in fact, requires that the illusion of separation remain intact and enforced. It also requires that our dependence on some seeming external teacher, as well, be maintained. Essentially, organized religion is little more than "spiritual politics", another level of control implemented by the illusory ego identity.

Now, if the ego identity was a local or personal phenomenon, this would all seem quite diabolical. However, the ego identity is not a personal phenomenon; it is a universal phenomenon being experienced as many personal phenomena. As I stated earlier, there is only one mind, one ego, and one Spirit that appear to comprise this universe. It is the divided mind's idea of separation or individual identity that instantly manifested, like a virus, in an infinite number of thought geometries that embody the illusion of multiplicity. It is instantly present in its entirety – beginning, middle and end, again including every possible director's cut – simultaneously – and in that same instant, it is done. We just can't seem to stop watching the movie.

That which actually *is* Spirit rather than what we *think* of as Spirit, is the only connection to the internal teacher that exists. This internal teacher is the *human* experience of the Authentic Identity. In us, it is experienced proportionally to our willingness to recognize the falseness of the egos counsel. The Spirit, not the ego, provides us with the only portal of communion with the *Authentic* presence. That is to say, Spirit is like the *"undisturbed" reflector, and what it reflects is the "disturbed" reflection that imagines the thought system that spawned the illusion of separation and gives rise to our false sense of self.*

Being indescribable in human terms, I can only offer my best attempt of a description, from a human point of view, encumbered by the limitations and constraints of any symbolic language. When the initial idea of a separate self was cast, there seemed to be a presence of mind invoked into manifestation. Since no thought or idea can actually *leave* that which thinks it, there was also a neutral connection to this idea of separation that was invoked at the same instant. The mind to which I refer here is only the idea of what a mind is from the point of view of separation. It is an imagined mind conceived by looking backward from within an idea of a separate self.

This neutral connection is what is often referred to as *the* Spirit, and it remains unaltered by the ego thought system that sustains the duality throughout the illusory state of separation. Even though the universe hangs suspended within the ego identity's many geometries of imagined thought, the Spirit remains an absolutely pure connection between the Dreamer and the dream. From the level of human form, we, as humans, cannot correct the error of the ego thought system. This is because at the behavioral level of form, we *are* the problem. However, the Spirit, having never obtained to the idea of separation, can show us the illusory split but remains unaffected by its seeming presence. The Spirit sees us only as the IS (God) created us. The Spirit sees us as perfect and whole and without limitation. As such, it is unable to actually "see" the problem, having never subscribed to it.

Therefore, as humans, we cannot correct the error from our level. However, we can see the error because to us it is real, and we appear to be experiencing it. The Spirit, which cannot see the error from its level, can correct it because it remains unaffected by it and is in perfect alignment with the Dreamer or Authentic Identity. In this capacity, we are able to express the willingness to receive the correction but cannot actually invoke it. The Spirit can invoke the correction, although it does not subscribe to the ideas of the error. We can achieve this awakening by allowing the seeming self to express the willingness to have the correction imparted and the illusion dispelled. As long as we insist that we can implement the correction, we get to remain here and pretend to do just that, while exhausting a seeming infinite number of failed remedies trying.

We are like numberless drops of water that have been convinced to follow our own *individual* paths and believe we are, each of us, a limitless ocean unto ourselves. As individuals, we truly are nothing, only representations of an idea, symbols of a thought. Only by breaking down the barriers (releasing the illusions) that appear to separate us and joining together with our seeming brothers and sisters, can our present sense of limitation be revealed for what it is. Only this way can we remember that *we* are that limitless ocean *together*, not here, not in this place, but in Perfect Oneness in the Eternal Always.

Nothing that we pretend to know or acquire can do this for us. These things only serve to exaggerate the sense of separation we foster within ourselves. This "joining together" isn't an act of changing states from separateness to togetherness. It is the recognition that there is no separateness, and that only a Perfect Oneness actually exists in reality. The way we do this is to stop listening to what the false sense of self that extracts its identity from the world of separation and fear is telling us about our separate selves. We can then begin to *feel* through the Spiritual connection to the Authentic Identity – the identity that is no identity, but is instead more of a "being-ness". What Spirit is showing us through our spiritual senses is vastly different from what the ego is showing us through our physical senses.

My first bit of advice is "don't listen to me" and by all means, "don't believe what I am saying". Instead "find it within yourself". All of the knowledge is present within each seeming individual (via the Spiritual connection to the Authentic Identity), and it is there that you must find it. You will not find it in this book or in any book, movie, lecture or seminar. You will only find it within *your* ONE being. Not within your seeming body, but instead within the human equivalent of knowing, that is delivered to the imagined individual by the Spirit through revelation. I am not writing this book to answer any of your questions nor to "show you some new mystical path". That is beyond what is teachable and would be pompous and arrogant of me to even suggest. What I am trying to accomplish with this book is to expose you to the fact that the answers you have been previously given do not serve you. I also suggest to you that you look for the teacher that is always there within you waiting to help you awaken. If I accomplish my task, I will be but a signpost along the way. If I accomplish my task, you will not need me beyond that.

To awaken, the first thing you will benefit by accepting is that everything (and I do mean everything) that you have learned in the world of form is essentially useless. Nothing that passes for knowledge *in* this place serves any purpose but to perpetuate the attachment to the idea *of* this place. There is nothing here for you. There is nothing that you can learn, nothing that you can do to *improve* yourself. There is absolutely no need for any sort of "Spiritual growth", which of itself is impossible. These are things that the ego seeks.

How does something that is complete, infinite and perfect grow? To accept that these ideas even exist is to say that you are able to override and improve the Creator's work. It is to suggest that as a body you are more intelligent than *infinite* intelligence and that which the *IS* (God) hath wrought falls short. You are perfect, whole and complete lacking NOTHING. Therefore, there is NOTHING that you *need* to do, achieve, acquire or become. To suggest that the *IS* has created you incomplete and has charged you with the task of completing yourself, is utterly absurd.

When you sleep and dream, are the players within your dream required to transform themselves into some special form or accomplish some special task in order for you to awaken that they be set free from the dream? If they fail to do so, are they doomed to remain trapped within the dream or get condemned to some *dream hell*? No, they don't. Nothing is expected from the contents of the dream to enable the dreamer to awaken and the dream to be dispelled. There is no required participation on the part of anything within the dream whatsoever. However the participants of the dream may become awakened to the awareness that they are nothing more than figures within a dream. Once aware within the dream, we are able to release any attachment to any aspect of the

191

illusion for they no longer hold the attraction we once found irresistible. Releasing such attachments minimizes our suffering and determines the degree of peace that we experience while here in this earthly insane asylum.

It is all a fantasy of the Dreamer, as the dream itself is but an illusion and has no effect on the realm of the Dreamer. Have you ever, in the process of one of your so-called *sleeping* dreams, become aware that you were in fact asleep and dreaming? In these cases, you were able to do things that you might consider impossible in your waking state. Also, when things appear to be getting out of hand, your "dream self" can turn to you and say, "Hey, wake up", or your "dream self" can simply change the contents of the dream to suit its preferences.

In this sleeping dream analogy, being aware within your dream pretty much allows you complete conscious authorship. The reason that the universe in your sleeping dreams is seemingly easier to author than is the universe in your waking dream, is because it involves a completely localized "idea" being projected by what I would describe as an equally localized fragment of the individual mind, which itself is a fragment. Not a fragment in that the mind has actually been shattered, but rather a mind that is entranced by the idea that these seeming individual or localized minds are islands unto themselves. I'm talking about a mind that is divided within itself.

In this respect, the Dreamer of our waking dream appears less responsive to our calls to awaken. This is, in part, due to the fact that the dream, or idea of such a dream, exists instantaneously in the Eternal Always (beginning middle and end), even though, in our experience, it appears to go on for eons of what to us is analog time. It appears to be going on right now. So the idea is not to awaken the Dreamer, for the beginning and end of the dream were simultaneous, thus the Dreamer needn't awaken. The idea is to simply awaken to the fact that we are but figments within a dream that seems to be dreaming itself. A tiny fragment of presence has attached to this dream and has allowed the belief that this idea of separation has actually occurred and that the dream is real. It is as though a memory of the idea has come to accept that it is the thinker, and that the thought is yet ongoing.

We would do well to accept that we, our seeming individual selves, are projections of an errant thought system that is, for all intents and purposes, locked within a seeming stasis of self-thought. In this light, certain things that represent what we are and do, take on a new meaning. When we see that we are inextricably linked to everything that we experience and that we are ONE with them, we begin to see that our goals and our very will is one with everything as well. We cannot separate one's seeming needs from that of another, because there is no "one" and there is no "other". There is only the Oneness from which everything we think we know extends.

Only in this light can we know real peace and happiness, and only in this light can we know true forgiveness. Again, I stress forgiveness is not to pardon a transgression and make it real, but to accept that it never occurred the way we have agreed to believe it did. Therefore, there is nothing to pardon in anyone. The transgressions within your sleeping dreams never occurred, as did none of the transgressions in the waking dream. We are, all of us, perfectly innocent and pure knowing no blemish whatsoever.

We have never left our state of Grace as the only Creation of the only Creator. We are the *one* effect of the *one* Cause, forever ONE, in Perfect Oneness. I (the Authentic Identity, First Effect, *not Victor*), and my Father (the Creator, the IS, First Cause) are ONE. That is the point to all of this. The point of all this is not to have you read this book and send you off on yet another path to nowhere or to solicit some unrealistic or unnecessary change in your current personality. Instead, it is intended to free this current personality from the shackles put in place by the same self that fear holds bound to this false idea of reality. It is to free you from the *false idea of a self*. You need not change anything about your seeming self since all change is illusory and meaningless. You need only express a willingness to recognize that what you think you are and what you really are remain completely unrelated. Nothing that you experience here in the world of form has any effect on your true being. Nothing unreal can have any effect on anything that is real – ever.

When you can accept that this entire universe and all it contains, is but an idea of a thought within a thought, like a dream within a dream, then the next logical step is to release the equally imagined need for it to define our sense of self. It is only an idea of a thought that what you truly are, what *we* truly are, is having. If you can accept the insignificance of the body and its demands, you can see that there is nothing that is being done *to* you (us) that is not being done *by* you (us), *for* you (us). We are in an imagined relationship with ourselves wherein we have agreed to pretend that we are many and each one is independent of any seeming other. If we can accept these things, we will see everything differently – through a new clearer Spiritual vision. Even with this acceptance we still perceive an illusion, but now we perceive without assigning meaning, value, charge or weight to anything.

We will see our seeming brothers and sisters like ourselves, and with this eye of compassion we can see the innocence and purity of what is. We will see that each seeming individual has the same goal and the same yearning. We will see that the ultimate "destination" of all is the same – Oneness, Heaven, Utopia, Paradise or Nirvana. Whatever the name, label or ideal that is applied to it, it is all the same. It is the returning home of the prodigal son. In this case, we are returning home to a home we have never actually left, not in reality, only in this idea within an idea, this dream within a dream.

To some, this awakening process will *seem* very slow, and it will *seem* to take quite some time to adjust to this new paradigm and accept these ideas into action. For others, it will *seem* to happen quite quickly, almost as if they have been waiting for permission to express what they have always known deep inside. Either way, it matters not how the awakening process manifests in each seeming individual, only that when it does, the seeming individual will know a greater sense of peace.

As each imagined personality agrees to see the illusion for what it is, and that there is nothing to be gained from it, this seeming personality releases its attachment to repeating its seeming adventures through this dream/nightmare anymore. They will release the cycle of birth and death to which they have bound themselves. There will no longer be an investment in the agreement that there *is* a purpose to being here and that there *is* something to be gained from all of this. You cannot add to completion, you cannot add to the infinite, you cannot improve upon perfection. You can only imagine it as less and pretend there is a need to do these things. In reality, though, there is nothing to be done, nothing to be accomplished.

• Chapter Thirteen •

What now?

•

What do you suppose we do now? Do we just sit idly by and wait for some miraculous change to simply overtake us? Do we take up some cause and crusade for a worldwide awakening? Do we sever all ties with family, friends and society to disappear into the wilderness and become a hermit? Do we seek out yet another guru or teacher and sit at their feet and beg for their philosophical table scraps with the hopes of finding our enlightenment in them? Does all of this sound completely insane to you? Well, it should.

But wait there's even more ... Everything that we think, everything that we believe, everything that we have experienced is all thought-based perception, none of it is the "True" and "Real". There is nothing that we can do, nothing that we can say, nothing that we can change, nothing that we can improve, and nothing that we can diminish that will in any way affect that which is *True* and *Real*. So, again I ask you, what is it that we are trying to accomplish that we believe is so important? What problem is it that we believe we are trying to solve?

To be certain that I have been clear on this point, we can't get there from here. Because here doesn't exist. That is to say it doesn't exist in the way we have agreed to believe it does. One cannot get to the Real from the unreal through some action that subsists in the unreal. You cannot achieve knowledge of the Real through thoughts of the unreal. You cannot take the Real and fashion it into the unreal, just as you cannot take the unreal and fashion it into the Real. What I am saying is that you cannot transition from one of these states to the other. The only thing that you can do is to agree to allow the recognition of the unreality of that which is not real. You can simply release the unreal and all that will remain is the Real.

We all seem to want "Spiritual vision" and to truly "see" the Real, but all the while we want to remain hidden from others ourselves. If we are not willing to share such vision, then we will not have it for ourselves. That which we covet will be denied us by the very act of coveting. We suggest that we want this *new* life, but we remain unwilling to release the life that presently holds us bound and imprisoned. When you remodel a house, you can't put up the new construction until after you remove the old. You must clear the way for anything you wish to enter your experience by first releasing the experience that you wish to replace. It is never the reverse.

We never get to have two ideologies actively in place and then choose which one we're willing to give up. We can only serve one master. We can only be of one source. Even if the shifting from what we perceive as one thought system to what we perceive as another appears to be gradual. We must give up what appears to us as our security and move to what we perceive as the "unknown". This is what is often referred to as a "leap of faith". There is always a period of uncertainty when the ego identity goes through the motions of what it believes is self-transformation. This is also the case when we choose to release the attachment to the ego's illusion of separation we call reality to experience something closer to our true nature. That is because the paradigm shift of thought involved in freeing ones self from the ego identity's persuasive trap is no less uncertain. Here again, the leap of faith concept is the only reasonable description I can offer. What we refer to as "fear of the unknown" is not fear of the unknown at all. How can you be afraid of something you don't even know? What we fear is losing the known and having it replaced with something less pleasing to us. Even though the "known" doesn't work for us, it is familiar to us, and therefore we continue to cling to it because at present we still identify our "self" through it.

As I have stated previously, no participation is required on the part of any seeming individual within the dream. There is nothing that we need to do or accomplish in this false universe in order to "get home". This of course begs the question, "What then is all of this about paradigm shifts and leaps of faith?" I'm not trying to suggest that you need to shift your consciousness on to some new train of thought. However, what I am suggesting is that you simply stop listening to the endless stream on false evidence that is presented through your physical senses and defined by the ego's thought processes. As well, I am not trying to suggest that you need to replace your belief system or your faith with some new ideology. However, I am suggesting that you can stop assigning meaning and value to these beliefs that have been fabricated to give meaning and continuity to this false self and this false universe. All of our suffering comes from our thoughts and beliefs about our relationship with reality or more accurately our resistance to it. What I am suggesting here is a way to release our attachment to the blocks that keep our suffering in place and thereby allow us to release our suffering itself.

So let us take a different sort of look at the same old set of ideas, beliefs and experiences which we currently apply to the core notions of our seeming lives. We might describe our lives as a series of trials and tribulations that arise from a complex network of entangled circumstances and events all external to us. We might also suggest that these conditions arise in a rather spontaneous, or not completely predictable, manner. We may as well say that this is just "how it is" and we either roll with the punches, learn to protect ourselves, or get beaten down. Even a person whom we would describe as being on a "Spiritual path", would look upon these same events and circumstances and perhaps describe them as "lessons". Lessons that can help to lead us into a state of enlightenment if we just pay proper attention to them and as well assign the proper meaning to them. Can you see where this is leading?

Those that agree that we "live" more than one lifetime would as well suggest that each of these lifetimes occur to facilitate this same "Spiritual growth" toward some elusive enlightenment. Each seeming lifetime somehow serves some specific purpose in this massive puzzle or riddle we call life. Each one builds on the results of previous ones and each one inches us toward some imagined goal. These lifetimes are perceived as some sort of *test* to see if we have become worthy of "paradise" or if we still need *more* training and testing. Those that do not agree that we live more than once suggest that it all boils down to one single decision. If we make this decision before the lifetime ends, we are accepted into the folds of some perceived paradise. If we fail to do so, we end up in some horrible place of eternal torture, torment and suffering. Either way, for those who accept that there is something more than this life, this life is the means by which we either receive whatever that "more" is, or the means by which we are denied it.

So, under the umbrella of these old ideas, it would seem that each of our days is filled up with several of these little tests or lessons. Depending on how we perform determines if we had a "good" day or a "bad" day. In like fashion, these good days and bad days add up to determine if we had a good year or a bad year. Ultimately, these all add up to pronounce our success or our failure in whether we had a good life or a bad life. To one group, the good life implies advancement toward the final goal, and a bad life means little or no advancement occurred. Additionally, in the event of a really bad life, some backsliding may have occurred. To the other group, a good life means the reward of eternity in utopia or paradise is received. A bad life, as I just stated, results in an eternity of suffering and torture.

So now lets take that "new" look at these old ideas – our lessons, our day-to-day experiences and our lives. There is only one lesson (if I must use this term lesson at all) that we seem to be confronted with time and time again. There is only one lifetime that we are living time and time again. There is only one day that we are repeating time and time again. Literally, there is but one instant we seem to experience over and over. The mind dresses this one instant up in numberless garments or images and gives them numberless names and creates the illusion of numberless events that have been enshrouded in numberless circumstances. The ego thought system perceives these all as real, unique and independent one from the other. Under the ego's influence, we are agreeing to believe that these seemingly numberless window dressings are some kind of path leading to some main event. We are agreeing to believe that they, in fact, occur in a sequential fashion and that each one is the product of the previous, and each one effectively dictates the content of the one to follow. What we fail to see is no matter what value we place on them they are still essentially meaningless.

Every Spiritual and philosophical discipline, that I know of, acknowledges the series of trials and tribulations we experience. Each has their own descriptions of the meanings of these events, but one thing remains consistent amongst them. Each suggests that they are presented to us as an aid in some sort of Spiritual advancement and that they are a series of separate and distinct events. Whether they are perceived as lessons or tests or mystical windows into the unknown, they are still seen as a series. If we are to accept that these tests or lessons arise from the conditioned world of form, then they can offer us nothing more than a view of the conditioned world of form in exchange for our dedicated participation. That is to say, if they arise from a state of separation they can only reflect a state of separation. You cannot take out of a bag that which is not in the bag to begin with. A map cannot lead us to a place that is not on the map. Likewise, if we are to accept that these lessons arise from the absolute, then it is through the influence of the conditioned world of form that they appear to us as they do – separate. That is to say, if this seeming series of events is in fact singular in nature, then any appearance of multiplicity is purely imagined. In this case we would be best served by seeing the common thread that gives rise to them all – which is the quality of our understanding *of* the moment *in* the moment.

Where these seeming events are perceived as lessons, they are seen as incrementally leading us on some journey of sorts. It would seem to be a journey toward the idea of some self-perfection, or at least some self-improvement that awaits us for all of our seeming efforts. As I stated previously, any belief in self-improvement can suggest only one of two ideas. Either the creation is more powerful than the Creator and is thus able to override the Creator's authority and reengineer the creation based on some worldly knowledge (deemed superior) of what the creation is supposed to be (rather than what it is). Or, the Creator failed in Its creation and has created us incomplete and lacking, leaving it in our hands to finish the Creator's work. Both of these notions are not only absurd, but they are an insult to even the most basic of intelligence.

If in fact, what I present here is accurate, then we are already perfectly one with the Creator. If, in fact, the Creator is infinite and limitless, this would imply that we as well must also be infinite and limitless. Therefore, if we are infinite and limitless, what exactly is it that we could really learn from *any* seeming lesson? How would it be possible for us to improve or change that which we are? As I mentioned earlier, it's not possible to add to, or subtract from, the infinite. So if there are, in fact, any lessons to learn, they must surely apply only to the limited or conditioned realm of the world of form. They apply only to the place in which they are deemed as necessary and are sought to be acquired. The only thing we can truly learn about the conditioned world of form is that it is the conditioned world of form and not our true "home". Since the only reality resides entirely in the absolute, then the conditioned world of form, as I have repeated, is but an idea within an idea, a thought within a thought. It's not what we *are*; it is what we are *experiencing*.

Since there can be no real knowledge of the absolute that arises from the imagined, nothing we learn from the realm of form has any real or direct bearing on the absolute. Since the only thing we can truly learn from the illusion is that it is an illusion, then all of the so-called lessons here in this imagined place are in fact one and the same lesson. What I am getting at here is that there aren't a series of lessons that we are being given, but instead there is but one lesson that appears to be repeated over and over in countless little disguises until we get it. There is but one lesson – period. As we apprehend it, the ego identity and its idea of linear time make this single idea of a lesson appear to us as though it were a multitude of different lessons (or tests). This one lesson is simply the Authentic Identity nudging, so-to-speak, the seeming individuals (mistaken identities) to come to the awareness of our Perfect Oneness, to awaken to our true being-ness.

So every single lesson we appear to be given is really just the same one lesson that, through the ego identity's images, appears to us as a new and unique lesson with each iteration we project. The idea that *is* the ego identity always projects a state of complexity. Therefore, the ego makes this one lesson appear to be numberless lessons that are all separate and unique that somehow must fit together to fulfill some grand puzzle or riddle. It is only another seeming function of the illusion that makes them seem as they do, and this is why there is no solution to the riddle or mystery of what appears to be our life here in the world of form. As long as we listen to the ego's guidance (what we call our human thinking), we will appear to remain submerged in this false universe trying to *learn* our way out. As you may well have guessed by now, this is a completely futile endeavor.

Where these seeming events are perceived as tests, pretty much the same scenario plays out as described above. However, in this case, rather than trying to "learn" our way out, we appear to be trying to "earn" our way out. As though by passing enough of these seeming tests, we will prove our worthiness to be "let" out of this "training-ground" and into "paradise". Just as I stated in the previous paragraphs, if there are in fact any tests (or lessons) to be surpassed, they relate only to the realm of the conditioned, and have no meaning in the absolute. Either way, if we perceive these to be lessons or tests, we agree that we are given numerous chances to prove, either our readiness or worthiness to move on to the next phase of our "training", or our lack of readiness that justifies our "failure" to advance. It's like we somehow have come to accept that we are in some kind of "boot camp" *leading* to "Godship". If the Creator is omnipotent and omniscient, then what sense would there be in creating an unworthy half-wit offspring that requires training and testing to measure-up to its birthright. Suffice it to say, there is only one lesson (or test if you prefer), and that is: "are we willing to awaken to Truth, or are we going to cling to, and suffer with, our illusions?"

Please note the word "willing" used here, as I never suggested that you *need* to figure out what the Truth is, only that you be willing to receive it. As I stated before, there is nothing that you need to do or accomplish (nor is there anything you *can* do or accomplish) and nothing that you need to acquire. Just offer the willingness to be shown what you already are and what you always have been, rather than dreaming to be what you are *not* and what you could *never* truly be. No active participation is required on your part. However, if you wish to

207

experience peace while here in this worldly asylum, a little cooperation in the form of willingness will go a long way. If you want to live out your remaining time in this asylum as a Buddha consciousness, sharing in the Christ Mind (or whatever you want to call it) then a more complete willingness is in order. Yet, no willingness is necessary at all as there is no condition that stems from the unreal that can have any genuine affect on the Real. There is nothing that you can do, or fail to do, that can change what truly is. The only thing the perception of self-transformation will determine is the degree to which we imagine peace or suffering during the equally imagined time we agree to believe we are spending here in the world of form.

Speaking of living out some imagined time here in the asylum; let's take a look at this so-called life. Because of what it is that I am expressing here, I won't be addressing the philosophy of a single life. That will be addressed a little later. As for the belief in multiple lives, well, that is another story. The idea of multiple lives is the same phenomenon as the idea of multiple lessons or tests, as I have described previously. The seeming numerous lives that it would appear to many that they live, are still just one life dressed up in seemingly different surroundings, with new people, new names and new faces. But in reality there is no life, no surroundings, no people, no names or faces. There is only the idea of these things. We continuously disguise them (filter them through the ego identity) in new appearances and pass them off to the consciousness as though they are new experiences, when in fact, they are the one and only experience over and over – separateness.

Dressed up as different periods of an imagined history in different cities and different countries, the ego identity distracts us from recognizing what is right in front of us all of the time. We don't see it because we are being dazzled by the seeming multitude of various objects that occupy our every human thought. We are so busy trying to account for what it is that we are experiencing, that we fail to notice that all of our thought is bound up in the past and/or in the future passing judgment against the "now". Even when we claim to be "living in the now", we are still experiencing a now that is inextricably locked into a past *idea* of the now. The ego process serves only to dissect and separate the one idea of what a self is. It pretends to isolate, define and label its seeming parts. All the while it appears to be doing this, it imagines the forefront or leading edge moment of its own expression into the imaginary, as the NOW. Nothing in this false universe is in the NOW. Everything here in this imaginary place is of the past. Like the DVD analogy earlier, this entire universe and every action therein is "in the can" so-to-speak. The beginning, the duration, and the end, including every possible "directors cut", are all contained in the same instant, the same idea.

As for the days that we appear to experience, they are the same as the seeming lives themselves. The same day is again simply dressed up in what appears to us as different circumstances and events as a sort of continuation of yesterday. This perception remains consistent at all resolutions. It doesn't matter how large or tiny the seeming cross section that is taken, it always remains the same. It is only our apprehension or perception of it that seems to differ. Large or small, it is still just a symbol of the one idea that is separation. We have simply agreed to believe that it has more than one meaning and that it takes on more than one form. We can ignore or distort the Truth in the mind, but we cannot change it. Nothing we do can ever *change* the Truth, only our *perception* of it can appear to change.

So you can see, as long as we view our seeming lives as real and starting at a given point, passing through a series of points and ending at some point, we will continue to believe that there is real value in what we accomplish during this imagined interim. We will also be inclined to view our environment and others within it, as either resistance or assistance to our progress and ultimately to our success. Either way, we will see our gain as needing to come at the expense of another's loss. Some might disagree with this idea, saying that those that are cooperating with us are being "compensated" in some way. Perhaps we are either "paying" them or, in some other way, they are extracting what they see as having "value" for their cooperation. This is only splitting hairs as to the level of resolution the ego thought system is using to disguise itself.

If we are rewarding them for their cooperation, we are supporting their belief in lack and limitation and the fears they engender. We are suggesting that we ourselves will benefit from their services, and that they, as well, will benefit from providing such benefit. Each of us appears to be extracting something of value from the other. Something that we perceive as filling some lack that we believe exists in our imagined self or in the conditions we apply to our seeming self or the environment that we believe supports us. The point that I am trying to make here is that, one way or another, we are attempting to extract something from these interactions that we see as having value in the world of form beyond what the interaction itself provides us simply through its being. I am not suggesting that we not cooperate one with another, but that we examine the motives that relegate our actions within any seeming relationship (usually selfishness). In other words, be helpful not because you will be rewarded or revered, but because it's helpful. Also, do not reward your brother because he was helpful, but instead reward him because the reward itself is helpful. Whatever it is you have to offer in order to be helpful, offer it without consideration of personal gain or reward.

If we can just release the need to consider each other as a means to an end and begin to see each other as an end to the means, we would begin to heal.   The means being the seeming process perpetuating the idea of separation – the ego identity. Again, this so-called means is singular in nature but representing as a multiplicity. It takes on numberless forms like gender, race, creed, color, national origin, political inclination, organized religion, and social status to name just a few. All of these self-imposed conditions affect a sense of separation and engender an "*us* and *them*" mentality. The most damaging of those mentioned is organized religion (in my opinion), not because of any overt atrocities (although there have been many), but more the clandestine agenda that it imposes. Religion suggests the continuation of the "separate self" into eternity, and this is appealing to the ego identity more than any other single prize that we can imagine.   The others only offer the promise of small scale localized and temporal power that ends with the seeming death of the individual. Continuation of the self into eternity supports and validates the idea of Godliness being applied to the ego identity.   It is confirmation that it is real and worthy of having been placed in the seat of authority by us as a surrogate for our relationship with Source.

By convincing us that we are a "self" and that this "self" can and will be preserved into eternity only by applying the appropriate cooperation, religion owns our devotion.   We are relinquishing any and all presence in what we perceive as our own life, out of fear. As long as we agree to believe that we are a self and that this self needs preserving, there is no way to release our attachment to the ego identity. We cannot release the self out of fear, as it is fear that keeps us attached to it. We are lead to believe that such an act means certain death, destruction and damnation for all eternity for this imagined self. It is not the death, destruction or damnation, nor the eternity to which we subject all of these conditions that fuels our fears. It is the idea that it will be imposed upon the self we invented to master and avoid these seeming pitfalls that fills us with fear. It is this imaginary self that is the source of all of our fears. We fear what may happen to this idea of self or what may become of it if we don't protect it at ALL cost. We lose any awareness of the true nature of the Authentic Identity to the illusion with which we have replaced it. We have become the lie that proclaims its "self" to be the truth, the darkness that calls itself the light. As seeming individuals we are, each of us, simply an idea of a thought within a thought within a thought that has mistaken itself for the thinker.

In an uninvestigated life we spend almost all of our time mesmerized with the conditioned nature of the unreal. This is because the conditioned requires this extensive (complex) framework of support with its delicate balance of interactions just so it will *appear* to exist. We just keep marveling at the framework, never stopping to consider just what it is that it supports. Let's step back for a moment and consider the absolute, which requires *nothing* in order to be a perfect unity. In a perfect unity, the existence of a distinct and separate self is not possible. The only way a *self* can exist is in relationship to something that is *not self,* and thus precludes a unity. If there is nothing that is not self, then there as well can be no inherent sense of self. If there *were* a separate and independent self, then, first of all, this would destroy any possibility of oneness or perfect unity. Also, this would suggest that whatever the Creator is conceived to be is not infinite, but limited. In other words, it would contain everything except for the separate self. It would end where this supposed separate self began. If you suggest that this "separate" self takes its existence within the Creator, then it wouldn't be a "separate" self. It would be an integral presence and any ideas of separation would again be purely imaginary.

This independent self stands in testimony to its own existence. It does this by collecting information from what it believes to be outside of itself and compares it to itself. The "self" has come to rely completely on the feedback of our physical senses for virtually all understanding of its every experience. Since these physical senses are actually a part of the illusion they stand in proof of, they too must conform to its parameters. By their very nature, our physical senses have a need to make "sense" of whatever information they're given no matter how absurd it may be. The physical senses must construct images and meaning that satisfy these basic requirements. This is how we continuously justify our experiences. No matter what it is that we perceive we distort it into something that conforms in some way to our present paradigm of acceptable conditions in attempts to set ourselves free. Yet it is the perception of this self-same paradigm which holds us in bondage in the first place.

Having said all of that, I would now like to close this book on a much happier note. As I have stated earlier, everything that we experience, no matter how profound, is nothing more than an artifact, a figment of the past, a reflection. It is only a tiny fraction of what we *are* that seems to remain captive in the memory of what was but an idea of a split instant. You see, we have already "succeeded", so-to-speak. It is only this seeming memory that is holding the illusion in focused manifestation. Its beginning was also its ending – they are the self-same instant as there is only the one instant. We are safe at home in Source. When the memory of here remembers the memory of home, all of the seeming fragments will reawaken to the paradise that was never lost.

You cannot fail, be left behind, or be forgotten, because you are *all* that is. The Will of that which created us (the Authentic Identity) cannot be overthrown or circumvented, because we *are* that Will. The Kingdom of Heaven cannot be denied us, because we *are* that Kingdom. We cannot "learn" our way in and we cannot "earn" our way in. We need only sit calmly and realize that we are already *in,* for there *is* nowhere else. We do not abandon a ship that is not sinking, just as we do not erect a fortress where there is no threat. We "appear" to be here because the idea of separation *has* already occurred, but so has the correction. There is nothing that you need to do to achieve recovery or redemption, as everything in this place is already past. It's not *going* to happen, it already *has* happened (in a manner of speaking).

This is good news because what is in the past is in the past (again a figure of speech), and this universe is in the past. This means that all perceived suffering and desolation are but memories of a flash of an idea. There is no reason to continue to perceive time and remain in this memory, but it is up to us to be willing to release it. For as long as we attach to it, we will appear to remain captive to it. As long as we see something that needs to be fixed, we will have to remain in this memory (this dream) attempting to fix it. If we perceive a wrong that needs to be righted, a world that needs to be saved or anything that needs to be changed at all, we will have to remain here attempting to do just that. We will have to remain until we no longer see a world that needs correcting and only see that there is nothing that can, or needs to be corrected. Nothing is amiss. Everything is just as it should be. It is only our perception of it that is biased through judgment.

As I have repeatedly stated, there is nothing that we *need* to do and in fact there is nothing that we *can* do. It is what we have been doing that we can finally quit doing. We can quit attaching our identity to what we appear to be experiencing and release our need to judge these things as real and needing our attention. We don't need any special knowledge or understanding, and we certainly don't need to solve some cryptic riddle. Intellect and achievement only keep us analyzing and reengineering the framework of our dreams, but they will not free us from them. No matter what it is that we have accepted to see around us, no matter how beautiful or how horrible, we need only recognize that it is not our home. We are not of this place – this place is of us. It is our idea, the imaginings of a dream (turned nightmare), but it is not real, not like we think it is. And, it most certainly is not our home.

If we think that we must resist or fight against this idea, then we make it real and we must do just that. When we agree that this idea is meaningless and holds no truth for us, releasing it will become completely natural and attachment will then seem absurd to us. As you sit there right now, you could have the idea of jumping from a high cliff. Unless you attach to that idea, act on it and make it real, it has no control over you and bears no threat or danger. It is just an idea and nothing more.

Imagine that ....

www.ingramcontent.com/pod-product-compliance
Lightning Source LLC
Chambersburg PA
CBHW060920040426
42445CB00011B/707